The Un
A quiet uprising

An existentialist memoir

Hogan Sinclair

Hauxwell Publishing

Printed in the United States of America

First Printing, 2013

ISBN: 978-1-907038-04-4

Hauxwell Publishing

www.hauxwellpublishing.co.uk

enquiries@hauxwellpublishing.co.uk

Edited by Simon Thackeray

For Mum & Dad

1. BACK-STORY

If I ever die a newsworthy death, make sure it's a good photo that's given out to the press. Don't be hasty and just give out the first clear head shot you find. Think about it carefully. That photo could be around for a long time, and it could give out an impression of me that just isn't true. I know I often look like a tart when I get dressed up for a night out, but I'm going to start toning it down. I've been saying that for a few years now, but it's time I started dressing more my age. But the photo thing's important.

I was looking up the media reports on a drug dealer I knew, who was gunned down outside his house, and he looks fantastic in the photo in the papers (obviously, there are no photos of him actually shot). He's all tanned and smiling. It's probably his wedding or honeymoon picture. But he didn't actually look like that. He had really bad acne.

This isn't going to flow neatly like the pages of a book with a proper structure. Real life isn't like that. People don't think like that. You're just going to get the ramblings from inside my head and my brain jumps all over the place. It's as good a place as any to start, so I'll tell you all about my childhood and what made me the way I am. I think that's important, well sociologists usually do. They want to know your "politics" or what perspective you're coming from. You can decide for yourself.

This is a kind of memoir, not a novel, so don't be expecting a plot because there isn't one. This is my etching on the cave wall. I'm writing this to leave behind a bit of me, which I now know to be entirely pointless. If I designed a magnificent building, I'd be lucky if it stood for a couple of hundred years. Even the ancient Buddhist Pillar, the 80ft-tall Minaret of Chakari in Kabul, which managed to last for 1000 years, was eventually destroyed in 1998. But I'm writing this anyway, which is ironic because I'm not religious. I view needing religion as an inability to accept your own immortality; yet still I cling on to the hope of leaving something of myself behind.

If these words are ever reviewed, no matter how shredding the response to them, I'll be delighted. If not, I've fulfilled a life's ambition just by using the word 'existential' in the subtitle. Seriously though, I suppose this book is about my disappointment with existence; with *my* existence.

Yes, I sound angry and disillusioned throughout it, because I am at times. It has taken me forty years to realise that I fell for *The Biggest Lie.* I mean, I should have known. The signs – the smaller lies - are there since we are little, with the Tooth Fairy, Santa Claus and God. The last two are cleverly said to be constantly watching your every move to make sure you are "good enough" to receive what you deserve.

I've been waiting all this time for my life to get better. I now realise it won't. I'll never be important, or rich, or beautiful, or talented. My existence will largely go unnoticed. My life won't "mean" anything. At the end, if I'm lucky, there might be an adequate turn out at my funeral and a lacklustre rendition of "Bind

Us Together Lord" and a sit-down tea with a sausage roll and a cake in a local bowling club afterwards.

I think I started to realise this – the futility of life - when my dad died. Up until then, I was still in what I now think of as "striving" mode, where you think you have a life goal or two that you're aiming for, even subconsciously. You think you're moving forwards towards something better, some point that you'll "arrive" at. It never happens.

I had been away in London for ten years, trying to make my life "better" doing evening classes and working on the trains during the day. If I'd known I'd end up back in Scotland, I wouldn't have bothered. I've been poor and fed up since. I'd have been as well staying put and working all hours in that kebab shop and keeping my little flat above the butcher's.

What an idiot I was, wasting all those years, working and studying. I'm worse off now than I ever was. Now I'm "educated", but still working class, I don't fit in anywhere. And to think of all those sunny days that I wasted indoors, reading textbooks, when I could have just been walking in the park.

By the way, if you're thinking about putting all your memories down into an autobiography, don't. You'll only be disappointed. There's not much there: just snippets, like old photos. It would be easier to go through some photos and try to remember what happened that day and to write about it. When you think back over your life, you realise how little you've done, that you've had no impact. It's all very depressing. Best just to keep your nose pointed forward in the furrow. Don't look up. Don't think too much about things, and for God's sake, don't think about the past.

2. JIM

I was parked, waiting to pick my daughter up from her friend's house, when I noticed three people coming along the street. The guy walking on the outside of the trio was holding a Spar carrier bag that was bulging with three big bottles of cheap cider. Right on cue, just in front of my parked car, the blue, two litre plastic bottles burst free from the flimsy, white bag and rolled away. The three people dived desperately after them, frantically chasing each bottle as though it was their own child who had run on to the road.

As they picked up their bottles and walked towards my car, I realised I knew one of the men. I'd known him since we were children. He loved me once. He walked past, his eyes straight ahead, vacant. I pitied his shaven head and hollow cheeks. I remembered how he got to this point and, in a second, back to how when we were young, he was still so full of hope. He was always so determined that he wouldn't turn out like this, like his mum, Becky.

At least Jim didn't have any children, brought up to suffer while he drank his life away. She'd had seven. Their house had an invisible but palpable, "do not cross" line all around it. The fence was broken, the grass was overgrown, the windows dirty, the blinds always closed and litter swirled around the doorstep. Neglected, like its inhabitants. The only money coming in was Becky's benefits and she drank and smoked all day long, leaving nothing for her children who, as well as having to endure this neglect, were viewed as social pariahs – a feral brood - by everyone else. Other parents told their children, in various ways, not to play with the McManus's:

"You'll catch nits!"

"She's got impetigo."

"He's filthy."

"They're stinky!"

"They're too rough."

"I don't want you going near them."

But there were a lot of them, so they were never short of company. My brothers and I were often considered "too rough" for the other kids in the street as well and our parents were often out, so we played with whom we liked. I liked the McManus children, but their mother was unpredictable.

Becky was a familiar figure in our street, traipsing unsteadily up and down the cul-de-sac, to and from the off-licence to her paint peeled front door, in her dirty old blue coat and ripped tights (when she wore any); her straggly, grey hair dripping down her back. She'd have sent the kids to the shop for her cans of super strength lager if she could.

Often, one of her children would have the torture of shivering in line to be served at the ice-cream van, waiting in the rain behind their neighbours. The other boys and girls at the van would be happy to be getting a ten pence "mix up" of assorted penny sweets, crisps or ice-cream to eat, while the McManus child would make his or her way to the front and ask for a single cigarette for their mother's 10p.

Like the Little Match Girl, they could see all the goodies behind the glass while they stood starving on the pavement beside the van. Once served by Silvio (our authentic Italian ice-cream man), he or she would then trudge back up the cul-de-sac with the cigarette carefully wrapped in the centre of their fist, keeping the paper dry from the rain. I don't remember ever seeing any of them have sweets of their own. They were lucky if they had a piece* and tomato sauce or a piece and sugar to eat in a day. They usually had some sugar in the house. Becky took sugar in her tea. When she drank tea, that is.

Jim was the middle child. He was the first whose father was not Becky's husband. Maybe that's when his mum started drinking, when her marriage broke up. My own mum and gran remembered a time when theirs was the "cleanest house in the street". We'll just have to take their word for it. That family lived in filth as far back as I can remember. Their living room carpet

---

* sandwich

was black and tacky, as though the whole thing had been melted, a bit like the spots on ours, where bits of coal had fallen out of the grate and burnt it. But theirs wasn't scorched, it was tarred with dirt.

Once, some workmen from the council had come to do some work in the house, but had refused to do the job, saying that there was excrement on the bedroom floors ("and not an animal's", whispered one of the men awkwardly, out of the side of his mouth, obviously shocked by the unfamiliar degree of squalor).

I doubt it was the dog's either. When it wasn't out, getting run over, the poor thing was kept locked up in a tight space, in an airing cupboard in the kitchen. The sad animal spent most of its pathetic life wedged into a narrow gap between their seldom-used twin-tub washing machine and the cupboard wall, unable to curl up on the stone floor or even turn around. It only fitted into that tiny space because it was starved to a near skeleton.

Only once did I ever see the dog eat anything and that was a day when it had escaped from its lonely prison long enough to wolf down some lard from the greasy chip pan, which was lying on the kitchen floor.

If it died, they would just get another dog and name it "Gyp" as well.

If the RSPCA had ever come round, they might have done well to take the kids into their care as well, but they never did. Neither did the social work.

There were usually a few cats living in the house as well. One cat, a big black and white tom, got kicked so hard in the head by one of the daughters' boyfriends that it ended up brain damaged. Its head was swollen and hung to one side permanently after that and its head injuries left it blind. It was heartbreaking to see it clumsily roaming around the estate with its huge lopsided head and its tongue hanging out of the corner of its mouth, but no-one took it to a vet.

A baby even died in that house. He'd been born with spina bifida. Imagine the authorities letting a baby go home to *that* house with a hole in his spine. There were whispers in the street amongst the adults that the decision was deliberate: that "they", the authorities, didn't want "it" to live (with disabilities) and knew the baby would soon die if sent home there. I don't think anyone cared one way or the other.

No wonder that little Ben had been born like that: his mum was under age and malnourished herself. I remember going round to see her younger sisters and she'd be sitting on the back steps, munching on a lump of coal and drinking tea. Maybe that craving for coal was a sign of deficiency in her diet, but no-one cared or got her checked by a doctor. We all just laughed at her black teeth. I always remember her teeth. She ended up with her jaws wired together for her twenty first birthday.

By then, she'd gone on to have another two children by her bullying boyfriend. They had nothing either, those kids. They looked like those malnourished children from developing countries that you see on adverts for aid, only they were white. They had spindly arms and legs and swollen bellies and they were dressed in other people's hand-me-downs. When they were only three and four, I was looking after another neighbour's rabbit one summer while its owners were on holiday and those little boys stole the rabbit's Weetabix out of its hutch to eat. You couldn't make stuff like that up; that a pet rabbit living in the same street was better fed than those little kids. And that was only in the eighties.

Amazingly, thirty years on and they and their mum are still alive. She still smiles a lot, even though she now has hardly any teeth. The older boy is a "recovering" heroin addict (sometimes off it, sometimes back on, depending on how his latest relationship is going) but the younger boy has done really well, considering, working as a supervisor in a bottling factory. Jim is their uncle.

I remember Jim sleeping in an old Austin Allegro I'd bought to learn to drive in. He slept in it for weeks, in our back garden. He spent his twenty first birthday in that little brown car. He didn't even get a single card from his family. It was heartbreaking to think that they cared so little, but a birthday card was an unknown luxury when he and his brothers and sisters had grown up cold and dirty and hungry.

I remember it was winter when Jim camped out in the car in our back garden because it was snowing. He must have been really uncomfortable, squashed into such a small space in the front seat and trying to sleep in the freezing cold, but he never complained. His upbringing had toughened him up to the usual physical discomforts. I would take him plates of chips and beans when my parents were at work and he'd get out and stretch his legs and we would chat for a bit, but avoid the issue of what he planned to do. There was no plan. But he must have had some expectation, however unrealistic. I can only think that he had hoped for some miracle in which his family would transform into a loving one and beg him to come back. But that never happened. No-one even noticed he was gone.

He was fed up with things at home. Who wouldn't be? The living conditions were intolerable, but he always went back eventually, because there was just nowhere else to go.

Jim was a huge Smiths' fan. With a cheap kit from the pharmacy, he dyed his hair black and styled it into a quiff like his hero, Morrissey. I think that must have sparked his interest in hairstyling. He was full of angst too, but rightly so (not like Morrissey, what's he got to be so bad-tempered about?).

Jim always vowed never to smoke or drink. He was going to be "different". Once, Jim got a friend of ours who was a teenage skinhead (and who has since died of alcoholism in his early thirties), to steal a book on Tennyson for him from our local library. Can you imagine that? A half-starved, Smiths' fan, would-be hairdresser, wanting the complete works of Alfred, Lord Tennyson? That cracked me up. It still does. But maybe the son of one alcoholic identified with the melancholic life of the poet whose father was also an alcoholic.

But anyway, Jim's skinhead pal, not passing too much judgement on his choice of reading material, duly nicked the book from the library and then handed over the heavy, red cloth bound hardback of Tennyson poems to Jim. Excitedly, Jim took possession of this prized piece of forbidden culture, ran up to his bedroom with it and closed the door. There, I imagine, he was oblivious to the stink of the house, the noise of his many siblings and their offspring running around and shouting at each other, and the rumble in his hungry belly, as he settled down to read verses like this:

"Come not, when I am dead,
To drop thy foolish tears upon my grave,
To trample round my fallen head,
And vex the unhappy dust thou wouldst not save.

There let the wind sweep and the plover cry;
But thou, go by."

With new-found hope, he decided that he was going to go to Corby or somewhere in England anyway. It might have been Sheffield. Wherever it was, he decided to scrape together the fare to go to live with some aunt that he had never met, to try to escape from here, to *make* something of his life. That was the start of the end for Jim.

He had dreams of becoming a hairdresser. That might not sound like much to some people, but it was quite a big dream for him. The obvious route would have been to enrol in a nearby hairdressing college, but they'd have been as well offering the course to him on the moon! He'd dropped out of school and knew no-one who had ever been to college. No-one in his family even had a job. He didn't know the first thing about applying for a college course or who to ask about it and, even if he did, I'm not sure how successful he would have been, trying to attend classes from home. He would have had to go to classes hungry, with his hair and skin and clothes giving off the stench of that filthy house he lived in, and his teeth were a mess. Years of poor nutrition and no toothpaste isn't the recipe for a dazzling smile. He would never have stood a chance of fulfilling his dream of becoming a hairdresser while living with his mum. He obviously realised that.

He was so excited about his shiny new life in England. He talked about it for weeks, imagining how different his life was going to be. How for the first time, he would be good at something, get a job, be "out there", living and, best of all, have some money. He thought he would soon be able to afford his own flat. Anyway, it didn't live up to that. Someone stole all of Jim's hairdressing kit from the train before he even got to his aunt's. He had saved up for such a long time to buy it. I can't imagine how he must have felt when, after travelling for the longest distance he ever had, to his long-awaited new life, he went to gather up his only belongings and they had all gone. He didn't tell me this until he came back home a couple of months later, more despondent than he had ever been.

Before he managed to get his train fare back home again though, he had been in touch. I was surprised when he started phoning me from England every night. We had been friends for years, but I hung around with his younger sisters and saw him more as their bossy big brother until then. I wasn't prepared for him telling me he loved me, as I listened on the big chunky dial phone in the corner of our living room, sitting on the couch next to the telly, surrounded by my dad and brothers, watching the Kenny Everett show on TV. So I'm not sure what I said to that. I was a self-conscious fifteen year old with my own issues. How could I offer him anything when he phoned, homesick? I couldn't understand back then why he was missing a home where he never got anything, but I realise now that at least around here was familiar and that just makes it feel a bit safer – a kind of security, I suppose. Mine was probably the only phone number he had.

The Jim who came back epitomised the word 'hopeless'. His now stooped figure and dragging walk personified a person whose spirit had gone. He was a man resigned to his fate and nothing ever lifted him again. I was no use to him, either, while he was away or when he came back. I let him down as well.

I snap back to the present and to him and his two drinking partners. They pass the car and although I feebly mouth, "Hiya" to Jim from inside the car, he walks on, either not seeing, or not wanting to stop and talk to me. I look at the dusty dashboard of my old Astra and sigh deeply.

What is the point of keeping kidding yourself that things will get better? Jim had accepted his fate. I was still clinging on to false hope.

3. COMMON PEOPLE

I'd finally let my cousin persuade me to go with her and my gran to the bingo. It was like a gambler's paradise, walking into that club. To get to the desk to buy the bingo books and to get into the club proper, you had to walk through a jungle of shiny, flashing, noisy fruit machines that promised to empty your pockets on the way in. I had my membership details taken and we bought our bingo books before we were allowed to go through to the main hall, where the bingo took place. It was a bit like walking into a very brightly lit pub or club, with lots of smoke (back then) and drink.

I took in my surroundings, snatching glances here and there at the other players as we walked down the aisles to get to a spare table. Most of them were smoking Club or Mayfair fags, the cheap ones. Every available finger had a ring on it, sometimes two or three rings on the same finger. I saw a few saying "mum." Others had gold necklaces with their names on, "Debbie", "Chelsea", "Angie". They had tattoos too, names again. Walking past the backs of the chairs, you could see that some of them had names – their own names probably - tattooed just above their fat backsides, which were bulging out over tracksuit bottoms and hipster jeans. Why did they have their own names tattooed on their arses? Was it in case their boyfriends forgot who they were with, when they were doing it, doggy-style?

Chips and curry sauce in polystyrene trays sat atop the grey laminate tables, alongside pint glasses of cider, ashtrays, and bags of boiled sweets. To me, that summed up the place. "Am I a snob?", I wondered at my take on greater Glasgow's lower class, as they happily stuffed their faces and fed fruit machines and mini bingo slots, pound coin after coin, until the main bingo session started. I wondered how they could afford to smoke, drink, gamble and wear gold. I thought gambling was stupid. But there I was, with my main session book, flyer and link ticket, just as bad.

Bingo had always seemed harmless when my granny took us to play for prizes of bubble bath and perfume in the chapel hall. This was totally different. You could come here for a few hours on a night out and easily spend your week's benefits or wages. Temptation was everywhere. You couldn't come in or go out, go to the bar or the toilet, without passing rows of bright, flashing fruit machines. Even sitting at your table during the break from the main bingo game, you were encouraged to play their "mini bingo" on the little plastic boards, where you slid a cover over each number.

It couldn't have been more effective in parting people from their money, if they had simply turned each of us upside down on the way in and shook out the contents of our pockets.

The demeanour of people changed markedly during the course of the evening. At the beginning, they filed in, smiling excitedly. As the night wore on, they seemed impatient and frustrated, and then downright sad and deflated on the way out. I was just so thankful I wasn't caught up in a gambling addiction, I thought, as I watched my cousin getting her latest "fix".

She was addicted. She was only three years younger than me but looked really young. She had even been mistaken for my daughter in the past and was still ID'd for cigarettes in her thirties. She had a fixed grin on her face permanently and was on Prozac and, often, Diazepam for a "personality disorder". Her personality disorder manifested itself as a belief that she was the star of her own show (life) and that she was a multi-billionaire who could buy anything she wanted. I'm sure this came about because her mother kept her in a state of unreality when she was growing up.

Her mum was only sixteen when she had my cousin. They were so poor that they couldn't even afford carpets, and were evicted for not paying their rent, yet her mother always told her she could have anything she wanted and never,

ever said, "No" to her. Of course, there would be many times that her mother couldn't afford the toys my cousin demanded in shops, so there would be elaborate tales as to why she couldn't have them at that moment, but that they would be coming "soon". Being three years older, I could see through these lies. They were constant. I couldn't understand how my cousin could be so gullible as to believe them, but she always did.

Even though my cousin now had two children of her own, her parents mostly brought them up and still paid for everything, almost bankrupting themselves, despite working all hours to maintain their daughter's bingo and fruit machine habit. Her sons are growing up broody, angry and resentful, yet unable to express their thoughts about their mother for fear of tipping her over the edge into another suicide attempt. She has already been "sectioned" twice in a mental health ward after a number of deliberate overdoses, so her mother was as desperate as ever (just as she had been when her daughter was little) to appease her demands.

Despite this going on in the background of everyone working furiously around this adult-child, desperate to keep her happy (along with the drugs she had to take), my cousin is still a nervous wreck of a woman. She has the beautiful face of a much younger girl, but is always inwardly fretting, unable to cope with anything in life except following the numbers in bingo.

I see old men, standing outside the bookies[1] smoking their roll-ups, and thinking about the money they're wasting and how stupid

---

[1] Bookmakers/betting shops

they are to fritter it away like that. Do they really think that they'll win? They must. But I wonder how they don't realise that it's the bookmakers, with their shiny shop fronts, now on nearly every corner of the small town where I live, who are the only ones making any money from gambling. The thin, nervy little men stand there in the doorways, not quite leaving. They agitatedly swap their weight from foot to foot, their white sports socks in black slip-on shoes. They invariably wear bland, cheap clothes, all much-of-a-sameness, with their thin, beige polyester jackets and shiny, navy viscose trousers; their fingers and grey hair stained yellow, as though they've slicked the pollen from lilies through it like hair cream.

And I conclude how pathetic their lives are as I sit in my car at traffic lights, judging them. I do my best not to curl my lip up in a downright sneer at the stupidity of their wretched lives as they stand, encapsulated for me, in that moment in the shop front.

4. PROTEST

The seventies and eighties were a great time for a girl to grow up in, well for me anyway. We had a female monarch, a female Prime Minister, and my mum worked in a man's job, as a Railway Guard. She almost didn't get that job though. It was the late 1970s when she applied and although she easily passed the entrance test and the medical, she was livid to receive a rejection letter shortly afterwards. She decided that British Rail wouldn't get away with it. Luckily, the Sex Discrimination Act had just been passed in 1975, so all it took was a threatening letter to management about how she was being discriminated against and she got the job after all. I was impressed by that. In fact, that sense of injustice and the resultant victory must have had a lasting impression on me. Perhaps that's what steered me to studying law. The power of the pen, the threat of some law, seemed like a way to actually be able to change things. But things still weren't easy for my mum. She was the first woman guard since the Second World War (when women only worked on the railways because the men were off, fighting), so there were no facilities for women, no separate toilets, no different uniform. The practical issues weren't the hardest to overcome though. The greatest difficulty was the attitude of other people.

Until then, work on the trains was treated much like joining the forces: there were no female colleagues allowed to "distract" the men from their work. Women were not happy at the prospect of their husbands working with the opposite sex. The wives complained. Men and women openly criticised my mum for "taking a man's wage", as though she, personally, was doing some poor family out of a breadwinner's income. She was. Women were only expected back then to make pin money. It was an affront to society that a woman, a wife whose husband also had a job, was able to make as much money as a man. My mum rode it all out and carried on, juggling long shift work with family life. She preferred working to being at home with us. Who can blame her? Who wouldn't prefer sitting in the back of train (or the middle as it was back then), in a nice, quiet guard's van, feet up, reading the papers, rather than being at home with three boisterous children?

I also remember the miners' strikes. I was twelve and at first, I didn't understand why my mum put her loose change in their buckets outside our local Fine Fare supermarket, or why all those men, women and children stood around the streets, collecting money. My mum explained that the miners weren't going to work so didn't get paid and their families were poor. A whole year without wages and our family had two. I suppose we were rich in comparison for a while back then. We were one of the first families to have colour TV, a video and a microwave. But I couldn't understand why the miners didn't just go back to work if they needed the money. It seemed a bit silly for them not to go to work in protest against losing their jobs and wages, because while they were off, they had no job and no wages.

The railway workers and steel workers often went on strike with the miners. There was a great spirit of camaraderie back then. That was the last time that the working class, led and personified by Arthur Scargill, had any real power. But of course, they had no power. They lost their jobs anyway. That power was stripped away with those jobs, deliberately. The country no longer relies on nationalised industry for anything. But we have to remember how long and hard those people fought for their jobs. Those people demonstrated, and whole families went without, for the right to work. The people at the bottom, the lowest paid workers, wanted to keep working, even down those filthy pits that damaged their health. They wanted the right to earn money. That was taken away from them. That was the real creation of an underclass.

But who knows, even without unions, maybe we'll see a bunch of supermarket workers and petrol pump attendants come out on a sympathy strike with their fellow consumers one of these days, over inflated prices and poor wages. The only thing that has brought the country to a standstill lately has been gale force, "red alert weather", winds, causing chaos. The trains were stuck in the major stations and the motorways closed, showing just how weak our infrastructure actually is. Freak weather can bring the country to a standstill, yet its citizens no longer even try, no matter how disillusioned we get.

Do we need a charismatic leader of Scargill's ilk to rally the underclass? Maybe. The real trouble is that people no longer fear the threat of losing their jobs. There is no job for life nowadays to lose. People don't have the same sense of purpose in a role like they used to. Even if they have a job to lose, for many of us, benefits will pay a similar amount to minimum wage jobs anyway. People are so used to living around the breadline that being in work or out of work makes no real difference any more. That suits the government. People will only take action against the State if they are desperate and pushed to protect something they value. If, instead, they have nothing to fight for, if they are used to just getting by on the bare minimum, then they will lose sight of the "bigger picture" (and any thoughts of rebellion) and instead just numb their brains with everyday distractions such as TV, or drink, drugs, fighting and, for some, petty crime. It is very clever to give people just enough to keep them quiet.

Anyway, so much for Thatcher, the Queen and my mum smashing the proverbial "glass ceiling" for a girl – like me, or anyone - and paving the way for equality. It was all a sham. I forgot about my station in life. Thatcher and the Queen weren't working class and the newly privatised railway soon did away with all the train guards anyway, women included.

5. MURDERERS

My mum used to walk through the street with me, saying, "She killed her man" or, "He murdered his mother". The streets around here were never paved with gold, they were paved with killers instead. But although that woman who murdered her husband by bashing him over the head with a record player after a drunken row, and the man who'd snapped after years of caring for his nagging elderly mother and choked the life out of her with her dressing gown belt, seemed a bit bad at the time, I couldn't help but be a bit unimpressed by them. "Murder" sounded so serious. They just looked ordinary. In fact, the old man who'd killed his mother was by then quite frail himself and walked with a stick. He looked abject, if anything. It wasn't until I'd heard of someone I had actually known being murdered that the word seemed truly evil. And more so, because the victim was such a gentle, harmless soul.

Maureen lived in the same block of flats as my auntie Eileen. My auntie let her come in and sit in her flat sometimes, but I now realise that most people thought of her as a bit of a nuisance because she was an alcoholic. I know I keep on mentioning alcoholics, but this place is full of them. That's not my fault. It's just how it is here. Anyway, Maureen reeked of pee and stale fags and talked too much, but I liked her. She let me pat her dog, a beautiful red setter. I sat on the floor, next to the dog, in my auntie's flat, stroking the dog's long, silky fur while Maureen occasionally patted my head with her bony, yellow fingers as she sipped from a cracked mug. Her hair was dyed almost the same colour as her dog's, but hers had white roots. She was very thin, with bony thighs, even evident through her heavy brown corduroy trousers.

Their block of flats was directly across from my primary school, so I'd often go across there on my way home from school, especially if dark clouds gathered and I thought it might thunder (which was quite often). I'm terrified of thunder and lightning. Everyone at school thought it was hilarious that someone usually so tough could be scared of a noise, but I was. I hated showing people that I was frightened, but there was something other-worldly about the forces of nature creating such force in the clash of thunder, and such energy in the sparks of lightning, that seemed so powerful and scary. At one stage, the fear of thunder storms, and trying to avoid being caught out in one, dictated my life. Some days, I hardly left the street outside my own house, in case I was caught out by sudden storm clouds. I had to go to school, I had no choice there, but I would run to my auntie's until the clouds cleared and I could get someone to walk me home, so at one point, I was a regular visitor there.

When I didn't see Maureen for a couple of weeks, I asked where she had gone. At first, the answer was, "London", but when I persisted to ask why she would move there, my uncle Pete admitted she'd been murdered. Murder. This town was full of murderers. But that murderer was an evil murderer. How could someone kill such a docile woman? What could she have done to deserve it? I'll never know. "Who's looking after Maureen's dog?" I asked my auntie, imagining it trapped in the flat upstairs, starving to death, but she just shrugged and I was too scared to go up there. Adults just assume that children forget things and that they don't worry about anything, but inside, I carried knots of worries about bad things for weeks, when I'd cry myself to sleep, imagining how Maureen met her death, what her attacker looked like, but most of all, thinking about Red, her dog, starving to death in that flat and me not doing anything to help him. That was a lot of guilt for a ten year old.

I suppose I feel bad about a lot of things. Maybe it's because of my Catholic upbringing, but I've always had a strong sense of (in)justice.

6. ANIMALS

I loved animals when I was young, especially horses. I dreamt of owning one. I fantasised about it every day. Riding my bike, I'd pretend I was trotting along in the saddle and every kerb I bumped my front wheel up was a cavaletti, or a log that my horse jumped over. But we would never be able to afford a horse and I had no idea how to keep one, although I was convinced there was nothing to horse care after reading an out-of-date Pony Club Annual I'd got for Christmas. I just had to get a horse from *somewhere*.

One day, I thought I'd finally got my chance. I was walking to Main Street with my mum when a truck passed us under the railway bridge and, there in the dirty road just ahead of us, a horse's head fell out. Perhaps I should have taken that as a sign about how my life would turn out. My heart's desire was to own a horse and the nearest I got to that was a severed head, delivered at my feet. But as a child, you don't think in "signs" or Providence. You take things a lot more literally. Besides, there was a slaughterhouse in the town.

I'll never forget it. It was a perfect brown head with a white stripe on its forehead. I'd have called him Blaze. I wanted to take the head home, make him better. He was beautiful, just lying in the gutter, abandoned. That meant he didn't belong to anyone. It wouldn't be stealing. I could take him home. He could be my horse. "Mum, we need to get him", I said as I waited for the traffic to clear, so that I could retrieve the head from the road, but my mum pulled me away. Of course, it could have been a mare. You can't tell from a head.

I always had this feeling with animals that when they're dead, they're not really dead. They look so perfect and still so real. People don't. People look like they've had the life sucked right out of them. They look worse if they've been embalmed and had make-up put on them and they're lying in a coffin, all done up. They look like mannequin dummies. If celebrities want to get an idea of how they'll look dead, they should go to Madame Tussauds. Animals look exactly the same, but asleep.

But guilt, feeling bad, sad, being disappointed – I was too serious as a child. I was never carefree, or really happy, even when I was little. I thought everyone must be the same, but I've realised that most people don't really care about anything much. I'm not sure if it's because they're selfish; I think it's because they're stupid. They just don't "get" things the way I do. I've always thought too much, too deeply about things. I used to wish I was more "normal" and didn't dwell on things, didn't notice what was wrong in the world.

7. GABRIELA

I kept a dead mouse in my duffle coat pocket for a few days. At first, my mum thought she had saved it from our cat and had put it in a cardboard box in my room to give it time to recover from its ordeal of being hunted. But when I got in from school, I opened the box in my bedroom, expecting a lovely surprise, only to find a dead mouse.

My mum couldn't understand it: she swore it had been alive when she put it in the box. A vet explained years later that a cat will often puncture the neck of its prey, which does not kill it instantly, so that the cat can still have fun, playing with the fatally injured mouse or bird.

Even when I realised the mouse was dead though, it seemed a shame to bury it so soon. It was still soft and cute, so next day, I took it to school and showed it to the other girls in the playground, but they just screamed and ran away. How silly and girly, I thought, being scared by the sight of a mouse.

It wasn't until I went round for my friend, Gabriela, a day or two later, after school, and she told her nana about the mouse, that I realised it was time to bury it. Her nana was disgusted and told me to throw it away and wash my hands. My parents never told me to wash my hands. She took Gabriela indoors. I had to admit, the dead mouse was starting to smell a bit.

Gabriela's nana was funny. She was quite old and looked very prim and proper with pure white, neatly styled hair. She was tall and slim and always elegantly dressed. But she watched wrestling and boisterously shouted out encouragement to Big Daddy in matches, especially against Giant Haystacks. To be honest, those are the only two names in wrestling I can remember. I was never a fan. But it did show a different side to nana's nature, which was a bit unsettling for me at first, that someone so reserved could lose their inhibitions like that, just watching two half-naked men grappling with each other on TV. My granny would have been mortified.

I had loved going round to Gabriela's. She was very bossy though. She was an only child of a single mum, after her papa died, and her mum was an only child too, so Gabriela lived with her mum and her grandparents in that little flat, all three adults doting on her. She shared a bedroom with her mum. I was shocked the first time I accidentally caught sight of Gabriela's mum in her underwear as she got changed in front of us, but became used to it as she stripped off or put on her nurse's uniform depending on what shift she was on when I visited. And she insisted I call her Irene. "I'm not Mrs. Canavan", she scolded when I tried to call her that, "I've never been married." She acted more like Gabriela's older sister. I had been brought up to believe that calling an adult by their first name was disrespectful.

I can't remember much about her papa. All I really remember is that he made us fried bread then he got cancer. Well, not straight after making the fried bread. But his decline, from the fit man who joked and fed us hearty fry-ups on a

Sunday morning, to bedridden patient, was rapid.

Gabriela would tell me to come into his bedroom to see him, but I was too frightened. On Sunday mornings, when I called for Gabriela, I would now just stand in the hallway outside his door, while she went in to kiss him, "Goodbye" before we went out to play. Even the sight of the baby's beaker in the kitchen scared me when Gabriela explained it was for papa because he was too ill to sit up and drink. "Can I catch it?" I asked, worried, after I'd picked up the cup and put it to my lips, not knowing it was his. I didn't quite believe her that his cancer wasn't contagious and I continued to resist her pleas to come into papa's room to see him.

Not long after papa started drinking from the baby cup, Gabriela was off school and everyone from our class was walked round from the classroom to the chapel with our teacher, Mrs. Johnston, who was wearing the black veil that she wore so often. She seemed to love funerals. They suited her sombre personality. She always seemed to be mourning somebody, or something, perhaps. Probably the life she felt she should have led, because I'm sure she missed her calling in life to have been a nun. Dressing for funerals was probably the next best thing for her.

So we were taken to the chapel to sing hymns at Papa Canavan's funeral. Mrs. Johnston was without a doubt a Catholic fanatic. We had no less than seven RE jotters in her class. If we weren't writing out stories from the Old Testament or the New, we were colouring in pictures of Our Lady of Fatima, or doing studies of Saints. They had all lived such gruesome lives. My favourite was St. Francis of Assisi who wore a sack cloth – or was it a hair shirt? And he made friends with lepers. I only really remember him because I admired the fact that he was from a wealthy family and gave up his life of luxury to live amongst the poor. I couldn't help thinking though, that he could have helped far more people if he'd kept his fortune. I probably liked him because he was the patron saint of animals. But there were others who, like him, also bore the stigmata, but I think he was the first. I can't remember any others. I daydreamed a lot in her class.

Mrs. Johnston had once said I was a "bold girl". I was quite proud of that. "Bold as a lion" was the only phrase I could think of. For a brief few seconds, I imagined myself as sleek, proud and brave, then I realised, when she opened her desk drawer and pulled out her belt, that it wasn't meant as a compliment. As she gave me my obligatory six daily lashes of the belt on the palm of my hand, I realised that she thought I'd been cheeky.

She and I both knew that the belt didn't bother me. I quite liked getting it. The other kids looked up to me. Even the boys were terrified of the belt and just the threat of it was enough to make most of them behave. When they were told to come and get the belt, they would pull their hands away in fright at the last moment. Not me. I raised my hands up fearlessly and smiled smugly as I received the furious lashes. My palm did smart a bit afterwards, but it was worth it to antagonise Mrs. Johnston even more and to impress my classmates. Besides, that was nothing compared to getting hit by my dad at home.

I wasn't sure what to say to Gabriela when I saw her outside the chapel, but she looked happy enough. Not all sad and crying like I thought she would, so that made everything seem okay. I was relieved her papa was dead. That feeling of sickness and dread, and that "forbidden" room that he was in, next to the front door, and the fact that we'd had to keep quiet and didn't get our fry-ups any more, had changed everything. It had made me dread going round there. Maybe now we could get back to normal.

I was always jealous of Gabriela's exotic sounding name and dark, good looks. Her dad was from Honduras and, as if that weren't exciting enough to have a father from a country I'd probably never even see, she got to go there and visit him a few times. She had a signed photo of him in her bedroom. It said, "To Gabriela, from Papa Pablo". He was like a film star, his white shirt unbuttoned to reveal his dark-skinned chest. All I had was a dad who was parked in front of the telly every night, drinking beer. Why couldn't my mum have gone on holiday and had a fling with someone foreign and handsome?

Gabriela got run over in the last term of primary school. She was walking home with me and my brother and we got to the main road across from her flat. Her mum, Irene, was across the road, waiting to tell Gabriela when it was safe to cross. She shouted, "Hold on", which Gabriela must have taken to mean, "Come on", because she walked into the path of a Ford Escort. The driver swerved to avoid her, just as she too tried to run back to the kerb she had stepped off. The car hit her. Irene screamed.

Suddenly her nana was there too. Gabriela's shoe had come off and was hurtling down the road. In her shock, nana went running after the shoe, while Irene cradled Gabriela in her arms. My brother turned me away, crying, telling me not to look.

It struck me that day how ridiculous adults are: they don't know everything after all. How could Gabriela's mother have been so stupid as to call to her from across a busy road? Why did her nana run after a shoe? And how random is it that one minute you are running home from school for lunch and the next, your world is changed forever.

8. PATRICIA

I idolised Patricia and she tolerated me. She was my auntie and had been the youngest girl in the family until I came along. She was five years older than me and I thought she was wonderful. She was in a band with her four friends. They all had their hair permed and wore matching white jumpers with "The Lollipops", written in pink around the waistbands and black pencil skirts (but only when they were performing). They played in working men's clubs and they often rehearsed in Patricia's gang hut in her garden. They even had an agent. Some middle aged guy called Frank who did the Provident in the evenings. Sometimes, they'd be hanging around, waiting for him to finish his customers' rounds, before he showed up in his van to take them to a club. None of them played any instruments. They just sang ("harmonised", they called it), a bit like the Nolans. They often fought. There was a lot of jealousy about who was the best singer. Usually, it didn't matter, because the smallest three were all roughly the same height and they'd stand in the middle and the taller two would stand at either end. They formed a semi-circle on stage, Patricia told me. I was too young to see them sing in the clubs.

Frank unwittingly destroyed the band. They had recorded a demo tape that they were going to post somewhere and Frank arranged for them to have their photos taken for publicity. They were to be black and white shots. "Tasteful", he'd said. He got his nephew to pose in the shots with the girls. I don't know why, he wasn't even a singer. He had a stupid hairstyle but the girls went all giggly and said he looked like Nik Kershaw. They fought over who got to sit closest to him on the shoot. Frank picked Sharon out as "the best looking one" and most of the photos were of Sharon and the Nik Kershaw lookalike, sitting like a couple in the Duchess Park, whilst the other girls sat nearby or poked their heads out from behind trees. Sharon really enjoyed herself. The other four didn't. By the end of the day, they hated Sharon and Frank and the band broke up. Patricia has never sung since, not even at karaoke. Her forty-a-day fag habit didn't help her voice much, though.

After the band split up, she was back on hand with her usual advice and dressed me up in her clothes and make-up to make me look far older than my age for my first ever disco. It was a scary experience that Boys' Club event, run by parents. We paid our money at the door. A few steps into the hallway and a girl was having an epileptic fit in the makeshift cloakroom. An ambulance had already been called for a boy who was unconscious after helping himself to far too much of his dad's homebrew from the shed before he got there, and a girl was throwing up at the side of the dance floor as I stood and watched in bewilderment, dressed in Patricia's clothes as Wham blared.

Patricia died of hypothermia last month. She was forty five. She was trying to save money by not putting on her heating, because she owed money on her electricity and her card meter had been set high to repay her debt. The doctor said she had probably fallen asleep before her body temperature dropped dangerously low. She was found frozen and soaking in her own bodily fluids, a seeping brown mess underneath her on her leather couch. She had lain like that for nearly a week before she was found. Her two cats, starving, had clawed frantically at her face to try to wake her.

I was angry at the council for sending her letters about taking her to court for not paying her rent. They didn't check why she hadn't claimed her benefits for six months. I was angry with the electricity company who had set her meter so high that she couldn't afford to put on her heating. But most of all, I was angry with myself. Where was I? I had never even been into her flat until after she died. I went afterwards to help clear out the furniture and cried miserably at the desolate, austere room. Not so much sad at where she died, alone, but where she had *lived.* She had worked all her life until about a year before and she'd had nothing to show for it.

The walls were covered with an Anaglypta wallpaper from the 1980s, which had been repainted several times, and all of her furniture had been given to her by other people because it was no longer fashionable.

I found her glasses and wept. Even they – that she had worn constantly – were broken. How could someone I had admired so much have come to this? It was such a waste. There was nothing of her left behind. I searched everywhere for something, anything, that would serve even as a memento but the most poignant thing she left was the memory of her inexorably lonely death in that sparse flat. The space where she had been was obvious, like the outline of the shape of her picture frame where it had hung on the wall. Her death left me with an unexpected pit of grief.

9. TYRANT

School was a challenge. The teachers were either religious nuts, hated children, or were just lazy sods. There was the odd teacher who was nice, but that was usually because they were still young and new to the job. I only had one like that, in primary three. But the first two years at school were awful. I remember being worried in my first few days because everyone else already knew stuff, like the alphabet and I didn't. I quickly thought though that my teacher wasn't that great and that I could do her job better. Mrs. McNamara was a tyrant. She spoke in that grating, falsely sweet, babyish tone to us whenever other adults, especially parents, were around. Apart from that first day when my mum had to wait around with all the others until I "settled", my parents never came near the school. As far as they were concerned, we were on our own. It was just free childcare, somewhere to put me and my brothers, so that they didn't have to think about us for a few hours. Yes, there she was, Mrs. McNamara, assuring our mums that we'd be fine and dishing out lollipops and blobs of Plasticine like she was some sort of Mary Poppins employed by the local authority when in actual fact, she looked like Trunchbull in Roald Dahl's Matilda - a dumpy, little, freckled-faced woman with a wobbly double chin, brown court shoes and matching skirt. She took a sadistic delight in hitting us at every turn, with whatever object was at hand. She'd whack our tiny fingers with rulers or her special teachers' bulbous ball point pens and shout in our faces until we cried. She'd be prosecuted for it nowadays.

On our first school sports' day, the priest was there and some parents, so McNamara had on her syrupiest voice and was pretending to love us all. It was a beautiful, sunny day and everyone started running in and out of the toilets for a drink from the water fountain. By the time I noticed they were all getting a drink, the toilet floor was soaking, so when I ran in, my plimsolls slid across the terrazzo floor and I fell into one of the stalls, hitting the back of my head on the corner of the metal cubicle. My head really hurt when I went back into class.

McNamara was still outside in the playground, smarming up to the priest. The other kids started staring at the back of my head and saying, "Look at that!", then, "Can I touch it?" A queue soon formed, all my classmates wanting to dip a grubby finger into my head wound, but only a few got the chance as

McNamara thundered back into the class, slamming the door behind her, shouting at everyone to get back to their seats. As the other kids parted, her eyes fell on me. By now, the shoulders of my white gypsy style top, that had been my gym kit for sports day, were covered in blood. "How did you do THAT?" McNamara screeched at me, as though I'd split my head open on purpose, just to annoy her. "I fell in the toilets, Miss". She yanked me out of my seat and then slapped my upper arm, saying, "Get to the office!"

I was worried. Would I be in even more trouble? My head really ached now. But at the office, the receptionist was really nice and asked if I had any big brothers or sisters in school. My older brother was only eleven months older than me, so she paused for a minute, rubbing her chin, until I remembered my auntie, Patricia. She was much older, she was ten then. Yes, she would do fine. Patricia was summoned from her classroom at the other side of the school and instructed to take me home to my mother.

When we'd made the mile walk home, my mum wasn't pleased to see me. "Aw naw, no' her as well, I cannae take any more of this!" she exclaimed. "And look at your good top! How am I gonna get the blood outa that?" She was just about to take my wee brother to the doctor's. He had been playing with the vacuum cleaner and was looking into the cylinder when he turned it to "blow" instead of "suck". A load of dust had gone right into his eye. We were walked up to the doctor's surgery. We were walked everywhere back then. The surgery was packed. We had to wait ages on the hard, plastic chairs in that dreary front room of a house that was used as the surgery.

Eventually, we were called in. Scott sat on my mum's lap while the doctor rooted under his bottom eyelid for the dust with a long stick. Then it came to my turn. I didn't fancy getting my head stitched. "Don't be a big baby", snapped the time-strapped doctor, "Look at how good your wee brother was. Not a peep out of him when I fixed his eye." He was right. That was quite impressive. Scott had literally been poked in the eye with a big stick. I couldn't let my little brother beat me, so I took a deep breath and braced myself for more pain. Luckily, the crude stitching, even with the doctor's big chunky fingers, didn't take too long and I got the rest of the day off school.

It wasn't great being outnumbered by brothers. It meant my time-strapped parents treated us the same. I was often just dealt with as though I was another boy. When it came to haircuts, I got the same "short back and sides" at the barbers' that my brothers did and often wore the same clothes (have a look at our school photos and try to spot the girl). Our neighbour knitted our school jumpers. She had a knitting machine and, enterprisingly, sold school jumpers and cardigans to all the parents nearby. She and her husband also worked in the local chocolate biscuit factory and brought home the rejects. They'd sell them for 50p a bag too.

People bought and sold everything door-to-door back then – tobacco, carpets (I kid you not – some guy would knock on the door with a roll of carpet over his shoulder, and others would turn up with a mattress or a clothes pole to prop up your washing line); and there would be, "ten pence can-dy apples!" (that guy just stood with his box at the bottom of the cul-de-sac and shouted that as loud as he could); a fruit and veg van; a cheeky, extortionate baker who sold trifles with synthetic cream and even the odd person trying to get rid of some pet rabbits or guinea pigs.

I wasn't so much reluctantly boyish as an unconscious-of-tomboy. I was so used to be treated just like my brothers that I didn't think twice about wearing the same clothes and haircut that they did. I had a pilot jacket and a parka and wore trousers and trainers. I got a BMX for Christmas, the same as them. In many ways, it was a good thing. It meant I was physically a lot tougher than other girls. I thought nothing of going over ramps on my BMX or building rabbit hutches out of scraps of wood. I had a lot more freedom than my friends did. No-one ever wondered where I was or worried that I might hurt myself. And I was always filthy.

10. CONNED

I had Mrs. Ranieri for the last two years of primary school. All she did all day was flirt with the school's only male teacher, Mr. Valenti, who taught in the class next door. Maybe they just had a lot in common, both being Scots-Italian. In many ways though, Mrs. Ranieri was the best teacher I had. She gave us some great projects to do, like letting us bring our dogs to school. Mrs Ranieri even let me bring my pet rabbits to school. After the dogs, rabbits sound easy, but these were a whole litter of baby rabbits that had to be fed every two hours with an eye dropper.

Their mother had died giving birth to them. Her womb had somehow come out after delivering the babies, blood all over the dirty, concrete floor of the rabbit run. It gave me a fear of childbirth, but not lasting enough to put me off having children. I carefully lifted the rabbit and her womb into a cardboard box and took her to the vet, who said he'd do what he could. But of course, there was nothing he could do for the poor mother rabbit.

He told me how to make up a mixture using evaporated milk to feed her babies. At first, I stayed off school to do the two hourly feeds, but Mrs. Ranieri found out why I was off and told Gabriela that I was to come into school and she'd allow me to feed the babies in class. They were like four little helpless, hairless seals: three pinks and one black. The pinks would have grown up to be white rabbits. Sadly, they all died, one after the other. I'm not sure why. Maybe they got too cold. We had no central heating in our house back then and it can't have been good for them being shoogled around in a cardboard box in the freezing cold on my mile long walk to school and back. Or perhaps I fed them too much milk at a time for their little stomachs to cope with, or they just hadn't had any of the antibodies in their mother's milk to fight disease. I'm not sure.

After days of feeding them around the clock they had felt like my babies and I was very upset to have to bury their tiny little bodies. I made them a beautiful grave in the bushes near my house though and decorated it with wild flowers and berries.

Another great project that Mrs. Ranieri had us do was to study the lives of poor Victorian people from a mining village. Over the weeks, I felt as though I had come to know these people, having found out all about how they dressed, how they worked, where they lived and even what they ate for their dinner. I was really excited when I found out that we were being taken on a school trip to the place of our study project: the Leadhills. It was an actual place and it was still there!

We were all given a hard hat to wear with a miner's lamp on the front and then we were taken on a tour of the mines. We even got to buy some lead from the gift shop. When we were told we would be getting to find out more about the people we studied, I couldn't wait. Maybe we would get to go to their houses and listen to them tell us all about their lives over tea and biscuits. Instead, we were taken to a graveyard, "Meadowfoot Cemetery" and told to find the gravestones of the families we had each been studying. How cruel is that? Getting a child to feel as though they really know someone, then showing them the person's grave.

It reminds me of the time when I won a raffle and I was delighted to find I'd won a chicken. I couldn't wait to collect it. I'd call her Doris and keep her with my other hens, Henrietta and Ermintrude. I was given an address of the person who had donated the chicken and my mum took me along. I was puzzled when my mum led me into a butcher's shop and was handed a bag. "But it's dead!" I wailed, looking in the bag.

I felt as though I had been conned on this trip to the Leadhills too, as I traipsed around, looking for the names of the people I'd come to know over the last few weeks. Dead people. While I seethed about the futility of this task, none of my classmates seemed to be bothered. They were running about, playing tig, or sitting on the grass, making daisy chains.

I cheered up a bit later when I found a large shiny white rock with gold running through it. I showed it to a few of my pals as we walked back to the bus. "That's fool's gold", someone told me. Maybe it was valuable. "Show it to the teacher", someone else said. Mrs. Ranieri looked impressed. "Where did you get it from?" she asked, surprised by my find. "On one of the graves", I replied. She looked aghast. "You have to put it back", she said, her eyes widening, as though we'd all be cursed. I put it down on the grass near the gate of the cemetery. I couldn't be bothered walking all the way back. I'd never find the grave again. They all looked the same.

We went on to the Straitsteps Cottages in Wanlockhead and saw how people lived in the 18th and 19th centuries. It was interesting, seeing the rough stone walls, the wooden bed and straw on the floor. You got an idea of how cold and bleak life must have been. In the later cottage, you could see their coal fire range that dominated the entire room, with big kettles and pans on both sides, being kept warm, and the fact that their bedroom was really just a cabin bed set into an alcove in the wall of the room with a curtain along the side of it. There must have been no privacy in those days. I liked the old-fashioned dolls' pram.

The previous winter, I had donated my pram to Sister Stanislaus to give to a poor family who, she said, wouldn't be able to afford toys at Christmas. I had been too big for it, but it was still difficult to give it away. I was getting too old for toys and it was hard to come to terms with getting too old to play.

I sat in the bus on the way back from the Leadhills with my head between my knees because I got travel sick at even the sight of a bus. Funny that, with my dad being a bus driver who often had to take me to his work. As the wheels vibrated under me, and the smell of diesel wafted through the warm bus, making me feel queasier with every mile, I listened to my classmates chanting happily away:

Stop the bus I want a wee wee
Stop the bus I want a wee wee
Stop the bus I want a wee wee
A wee wee cup o' tea!

And

Oh ye cannae shove yer granny aff the bus

Oh ye cannae shove yer granny aff the bus
Oh ye cannae shove yer granny, 'cos she's yer mammy's mammy
Oh ye cannae shove yer granny aff the bus!

I pondered on the deaths of those people I had come to think I knew who had lived all those years before in Wanlockhead village. What a hard life they'd lived, all crammed into a single room, working long hours every day, and for what? They were all dead, just the same. I reflected on my own mortality. What would I grow up to "be"? I wondered. "Why am I here?" I didn't believe that we'd all go to heaven and live happily ever after. Was that just to pacify us, so that we'd happily accept this dreary life before we died? If Mrs. Johnston's stories were true, I'd never get to heaven. You had to wait years and years in some place called purgatory first, hoping other people still alive would say enough prayers to get you into heaven. They must be like savings coupons.

I wondered how many you got for someone saying an *Our Father* on your behalf and how much for a whole decade of the rosary. What happened if the people who knew you didn't pray? Or if they all died before you had enough prayers to get you out of purgatory and into heaven? Did all the prayers at all the masses and rosaries go into one, huge, central prayer bank somewhere and you got allocated an account as you entered purgatory? What did you do to pass the time in purgatory?

It was even worse if your parents hadn't taken the trouble to have you baptised. You'd never get into heaven then. My mum fretted about that. Her first baby had died suddenly, days after he was born. It was totally unexpected and they were recently (shotgun) married teenagers. My mum hadn't even taken the baby home from hospital, so of course they hadn't planned a christening. What kind of God would refuse entry to paradise to a tiny baby because his stupid young parents hadn't had him baptised? Well, they had also had sex before marriage. Maybe they were being punished for their terrible sin.

They've scrapped limbo now, at least in our parish. I wonder what made them change their minds. How do they even know God has changed his entrance policy? What happened to all those babies and other non-Catholics who were stuck in limbo all that time? Maybe they got to purgatory, but have to join the back of the queue. Waiting is still waiting, so what's the difference? Maybe they've got a better waiting room in purgatory. Religion left me with more questions than it answered but the adults just got annoyed if I asked them anything. "A good Catholic just believes" was the general consensus. I was definitely headed for hell then. I had far too many questions.

11. ARTHUR

Arthur was an embarrassment, but not at first. When he moved into our street with his mum and his sister, Brenda, I didn't really notice him. I became friends with Brenda. She was older than me and a bit old fashioned. She wore those long skirts from the seventies in awful brown or beige and she'd never had her long, auburn hair cut into any kind of style. Her dad was dead, so maybe they didn't have much money, but she was kind. Not at all bitchy and nasty when she got you on your own, away from the adults, like some older girls could be.

I wasn't friends with her long when her older brother, Arthur, started saying, "Hello" to me when he saw me out in the street. I would pat his greyhound and chat to him about the dog. My granda kept greyhounds and I often went out walking with him to exercise them. Brenda told me suddenly one day that she was moving away. I asked her where she was going, but she was a bit vague and just said she was going to live with her older brother. "Arthur?" I asked, "but you already live with him. You've only just moved here, how come you're moving again?" Her eyes widened. "How do you know Arthur?" she demanded. "Keep away from him, okay?" I knew it was something bad. I didn't ask her why. I never saw her again after that.

In the summer before I went to high school, I saw Arthur many times. Mostly, I just smiled at him and said, "Hiya". One day, I was passing his back garden when I saw him cradling a big black hen. I kept hens. I knew it was a Black

Orpington and I knew it wasn't his. I marched into his garden. "That's not your hen, Arthur, it's Mr. Dickson's". Mr. Dickson lived in our street. Arthur went on stroking the hen, talking to it in a low voice. My heart softened. "He must love animals, like I do", I thought. Still, you can't just take other people's animals. "You have to give it back", I said, bossing Arthur. He stroked the bird one last time then laid it in my arms. I took the hen back to its owner.

After a couple of days, I hadn't heard Mr. Dickson's hens clucking. I shouted over the garden fence and asked him where they were, "In the bin. I wrung their necks". He said it so matter-of-factly. He hadn't even killed them to eat them. He just couldn't be bothered keeping them any more. He'd got rid of them like a bit of rubbish. I ran round the back of our hut and slumped onto the grass and cried. It was all my fault. Arthur could have kept that one. Arthur could have had them all! I hated Mr. Dickson. Arthur understood. He loved animals. He couldn't be bad.

But no-one else liked Arthur. The other neighbours got a petition up to get him evicted from his council house. That's because Arthur had attacked a schoolgirl who passed by his house. She was walking home from school, idly pulling at hedges and weeds as she walked down the street, when she unwittingly pulled some from Arthur's garden as she sauntered along. His front garden was a total eyesore. Everyone else had grass. Not him. His was just bare muck with a load of weeds around the edges. I wasn't there that day, I just heard about it later from my mum.

The story goes that the girl had passed Arthur's garden and had walked uneventfully to the top of the street, not realising her "crime" until Arthur suddenly pounced on her and tried to drag her back to his house. She put up a fight but he pulled her so hard, he dislocated her arm from its socket. The girl's screams were heard and a number of men in the street ran out and grabbed Arthur who told them that she had stolen a plant from his garden. Somehow, they must have let him go and there was no mention of the police being called, but the adults were unsure what to do next. The men wanted to beat him up and/or to have him evicted from the area.

My mum refused to sign the petition. She argued that Arthur's old mother would be put out into the street if they were evicted and she didn't want that. I thought about Mrs. Maguire. She was a cleaner at the high school.

Whenever I saw her, she kept her eyes on the pavement and she always wore the same cream trench coat, whatever the weather. It was old and dirty. Her hands were orange from smoking and so was the front of her white hair. I don't know why they gave her a cleaning job. She didn't look very clean. I had taken round some fudge and three miniature jars of jam once, on Christmas morning, for her and Arthur. It took her ages to answer the door. She grabbed the presents and closed the door again so quickly, I'm not sure she even said, "Thanks". I did notice she had no carpets in the hall. Come to think of it, she often had black eyes and bruises on her cheeks. She was too old to have got them fighting. Arthur must have done it. He was getting weirder. He often wore a surgical collar. I don't think he needed it because he would wear it some days, but not others and he had it for such a long time. He wore the same purple, nylon tracksuit with red stripes down the sides for months, with or without the collar. The only difference was his hair. Sometimes, it would be really long and he'd have a full beard too, or he'd shave the beard off and his head so close to his scalp that he was bald. He walked fast, almost always with his greyhound beside him, big feet pointing ten to two. And his face was always set as though he was walking against a biting wind.

I remember we came back home from a fortnight's caravan holiday up the North of Scotland once and we saw Arthur, miles from home, walking along the grass verge, next to the hard shoulder. He had on his tracksuit and his collar. We laughed. That sight meant more than any road sign that we were nearly home. That old saying, "familiarity breeds contempt" was true of how the kids in the street reacted to Arthur after a while.

Some of the boys, bored after a long, cold winter, decided to make it a game to try and antagonise him into giving them a chase. They threw stones at his door and shouted "madman, madman, madman", from the corner of the road opposite Arthur's house. They were no match to outrun him though. He was super fit. He walked miles and miles every day. My older brother was unlucky enough to be the first caught.

I was in the house with my mum and younger brother. Mum was ironing. My wee brother was playing with his cars on the carpet beside me and I was just out of the bath and sitting in my nightdress, drying my hair next to the fire, when there was a furious banging on the front door. I stood behind my mum when she opened it. It was two of the neighbours, the mums of the other boys who'd run home in fright when Arthur had given chase. The women were falling over themselves to blurt out that Arthur had grabbed Johnny. They told my mum not to worry, that their husbands were out looking for Arthur and that they'd, "Kill the bastard".

My mum had barely closed the door, clearly unsure what to do, when the door was banged again and there stood Arthur, holding our Johnny up so high by the scruff of his neck that he was choking. He'd also wet himself. Arthur threw him down onto the steps and marched away. After listening to his sobbing story for a minute or two, my mum ran to his friends' houses to tell the women to call off their men, that Arthur hadn't harmed her boy after all. She was pleased. She felt justified in not signing that petition. She felt sure that's why Arthur hadn't harmed her son. I wondered if Arthur had spared him because he was my brother. More likely, he feared the wrath of the men if he was caught hurting another child.

I felt invincible around Arthur, sure he would never hurt me, that was until I had started high school. Just after I started, I took a short cut by myself along a grassy path that took me home past the back gardens. Arthur must have noticed me going that way. One day, as I made my way home on my own from school, he was waiting with his dog in a clearing some distance before the houses. I had seen him many times before, but this time, I was suddenly aware of my surroundings. There was no-one else around. That saying about the hairs on the back of your neck standing up if you sense danger suddenly made sense. I had this prickly feeling of fear.

I remembered the time he had the hen. I was alone with him then. My mind furiously scrabbled to search for a clue as to why that time he was so compliant. Was it the hen? I didn't have a hen, only my school bag. "What are you doing out here? Are you waiting for me?" I said as assertively as I could and marched past him, as confidently as I dared, lightly patting his dog's head as I went. Arthur's eyes darted around, as though he was figuring out what to do, if anyone was looking. I smiled brightly as though he was my friend and kept talking, trying to sound confident, nonchalant even. I moaned about my day at school, about the boring lessons and the bossy teachers. On and on I talked, walking with a quick pace, a smile fixed on my face. I kept up the pretence of being relaxed in his company, of being his friend. It was working. Arthur simply walked alongside me, quietly.

As we neared the houses, I began to feel safer, but my heart was pounding in fear of the realisation that I had been on my own with this strange and violent man, vulnerable. I vowed I wouldn't walk home that way again by myself. I started walking home the front way, along the street, down the pavement past the front gardens of the houses, just like everyone else.

I was annoyed with Arthur for curtailing my freedom. I had loved walking home the back way, through the grass and the trees by myself. That little grassy, tree-lined strip from the school playing field down to the houses and running alongside the bottom of the back gardens had been like my own secret little haven. I had loved being on my own and being close to nature. For the first time in my life, I was scared to go there on my own and I resented Arthur for that. But I only really started to hate him later on, when he made me a laughing-stock as well. I began to feel like a prisoner because of him.

It's bad enough growing up, trying to fit in, without some weirdo trying to be your pal. I was getting to the age where I felt self-conscious and I just wanted to blend in. But I couldn't do that because of him. He would crouch down under the window in his front room and wait for me to come into view and, as soon as he saw me, he'd jump up and start waving like a lunatic. The other kids noticed and teased me about being creepy Arthur's girlfriend. I was furious. I walked home on the opposite side of the pavement and would no longer even look in his direction. Then came the final straw. The idiot had somehow managed to capture a seagull. Have you seen the size of those things up close? They are huge birds. Well, he had kept it in his bedroom. It must have been shitting everywhere. Worse, it was desperate to escape and it didn't understand what glass was, so it battered itself against the window. The noise! It was so loud. That's what made me look up that lunchtime. I stood there, dumbfounded at the sight of the poor thing, although at the same time, a little bit impressed that he'd managed to get it into his room, but mostly just wanting to see it set free.

But it never got free. I stood in the street, looking up helplessly. The big grey and white gull just kept on bashing itself against the window, over and over again until the pane was covered in blood. I wanted to go right in there, tell him not to be so crazy, to let it out, but I was too scared. He might have wanted me to go to the door so he could grab me into his house. By then, I hadn't seen his mum for weeks. The seagull battered itself for the last time against the glass and slid down. I knew it was dead.

12. CAREER ADVICE

Secondary school was a struggle for me. I was so ill. I had Graves' disease, but no-one knew what was wrong with me. My parents thought I was just pretending to be ill to get off school. I ended up with huge, googly, Marty Feldman eyes and a thick neck. One boy summed up my appearance perfectly when he remarked that I looked like an owl. Because of my untreated hyperthyroidism, I was very skinny. People often assumed I was anorexic. My racing metabolic rate left me anxious and jittery. It's bad enough being an awkward, self-conscious teenager without looking weird.

After the operation, I came out of hospital with a huge scar across my throat. A wire stitch ran horizontally from one side of my neck to the other, secured at each end with a big bead. The wire was held in place with vertical strips of tape, so I looked just like Frankenstein, but at least I no longer felt like I was dying.

I had failed all my exams at school in the years I was ill, so I had been told by the school careers' advisor to leave because there was "no point" in me staying on at school.

Careers advisors! They reel you in with a cosy chat first about what you enjoy doing. Next, they press you, "But what can you see *yourself* doing, for a *j-o-b?*" They mouth the words slowly, to emphasise them, as though they are speaking to a retarded person. You're still not getting it, as you babble on about being a teacher, or a writer, or a lawyer. Short of slapping you in the face to shut you up like they used to do with hysterical people, careers advisors think they have no choice but to be blunt: "Well THAT'S never going to happen. So, let's think about YOUR options. Why don't you leave school and do a Youth Training Scheme?" A YTS is for people who are not very academic but who are too young to get a proper job. I announced to the careers advisor that I was staying on to do my Highers and that I would go to university. She gave me a look of pity, as though she thought, "No chance!"

Maybe, if I hadn't had that encounter, been given that "advice", then I wouldn't have been so preoccupied with proving myself through education for all those years. Well, I've certainly shown her that I can pass exams, but really, she's had the last laugh: where has it all got me? Nowhere. She was right: I'd have been better off doing that YTS after all. Maybe she hadn't meant it to be personal. She probably knew that there was no point in teenagers around here having unrealistic dreams.

13. USED

My first flat was a room above a pub. I shared it with a milkman and a serial rapist on steroids. Well, I didn't know he was a rapist at the time. He drove a burgundy Volvo. He was always nice to me and even took me for driving lessons at midnight. Maybe that should have made me suspicious, but I thought we went out at night because I wasn't insured and the roads would be quieter.

He bought all of his clothes from a designer shop and was really muscular, so a lot of girls found him attractive. He would go out clubbing from Thursday to Sunday and would bring a different girl home each of those nights. He didn't rape *them*. They came back for a shag willingly. No, he would go down the local country park, make out that he was jogging, when really, he was scouting for women to attack.

For some weird reason, maybe he got more of a kick out of it; he went for women who had children with them. Perhaps they fought back more, increasing his excitement, or perhaps he resented them because they were mothers. He probably hated his own mum.

I only found out all this stuff in the local paper after he was arrested. At the time, I'd pass him in the hallway of our shared flat, or meet him in the kitchen and he'd say things to me like, "Don't go down the park on your own, that was another woman raped down there today". Really, thinking back, I should have wondered how he knew when the rapes were happening, but I would just thank him for telling me. Ironically, a friend from school came to visit me, to see the flat, and asked who I was sharing with. I explained two strangers and she said, prophetically, "For all you know, you could be sharing with a serial rapist!" She had always been quite theatrical, so I just laughed. But how right she was.

The milkman was an old nuisance, always nagging me about something. I say, "old" but when you're eighteen, anyone over twenty five is old. He might have been in his forties or fifties. He was still working anyway. Of course, he had to get up early in the morning, so he had a lot to say about the noise my pals and I made late at night. I had been a total geek when I was younger, a bit of a loner, and into sitting around, writing poems and stuff. When I got to eighteen and had moved out of my parents' house, I started hanging around with an older crowd that I met through Spook, a guy who had grown up in the same street as me. They all took drugs and drank tonic wine. Not heavy drugs like heroin or smack, just the odd acid or ecstasy, but it was speed and dope mostly.

Thinking back, I now realise that they took advantage of my trusting nature and my need to try to fit in with them. Soon they were hiding huge bags of speed in Slender Plan boxes in our kitchen and large chocolate bar sized slabs of resin (dope) under the beds. The first sight of that much dope scared me. They left all those drugs in my flat, leaving me with the liability for it, while they made all the profit. Drug dealers don't care who takes the rap, as long as they don't get caught.

My mum lived next door to an elderly lady and suddenly, her grandson started visiting her all the time. (It was him I told you about earlier, who looked good in the photo for the papers.) It wasn't until he was gunned down and killed outside his house in a fancy new-built neighbourhood near Glasgow for something to do with his serious drug dealing that we suspected why he had suddenly taken a fondness for his old granny.

Not only did Spook and his dodgy mates store their drugs in my flat, but they used it as a doss-house for all their mates as well. People I didn't even know would turn up at the door. On Saturday nights, the flat got so full, I would be tripping over people in the hallway. Auld Wullie, the milkman was far from happy, "It's like fuckin' Sauchiehall Street in here! And I've got my work in the morning. Get rid of them!" He had a fair point. I was fed up with it too, but I didn't know how to get rid of them or to stop them coming. They joked about sprinkling Wullie's cornflakes with speed. He always left his bowl of cornflakes laid out on the kitchen worktop at night before he went to bed, just to add milk in the morning. I now realise he was being considerate and that he probably did that so that he didn't wake anyone up.

It was a blessing in disguise when the landlady called round one night, saw everyone in, and ordered me out. By rights, she should have got a court order, but after a tearful night, I was relieved to be moving out. I swore to cut all ties with these so-called friends from then on and not to tell them where I moved to.

They weren't real friends. They were the kind of friends who thought it was funny to spike you with drugs. I remember one night, staggering out of a car and having to crawl inside on my hands and knees, wondering why I couldn't walk after having less than a bottle of tonic wine. It wasn't until next day, when I got a phone call from Frank, asking if I'd had a good time the night before, that I found out what had happened to me. He burst out laughing and told me he'd spiked my wine with four Valium.

Fast forward twenty mostly uneventful years later, when I met Frank, in Aldi. He looked exactly the same. Well, he had the same hairstyle, only it was grey now, not brown, and he had his teenage son with him. As we both queued next to the conveyor belt, we chatted about what we were doing with our lives:

"Nothing, I'm no' working, havenae done anything for ages."

"Me neither".
"Where ae you staying these days?"
"Clayburn Avenue"
"Oh right, I'm not far fae you then".

And that was it. Twenty years of catching up and we had filled in our life stories in less than a minute. I couldn't get out of there fast enough. At least I'd changed my hairstyle.

Frank wasn't the worst of the bunch. Kevin was sociopath: he seemed to know exactly what to say to charm people, especially girls, but at the same time, was devoid of any real emotion. He stole off everyone, including his elderly grandfather who doted on him. He had held a party in his parents' absence just before I met him (they had gone to Corfu for two weeks' holiday) and seemed oblivious to their outrage at finding their house completely trashed (mostly by

Kevin himself), when they came back home. They weren't rich people. Having to replace their smashed possessions and windows must have set them back quite a bit.

One of Kevin's favourite fantasies at the time involved his only sister's wedding reception where, he vowed, he would spike all of the guests with LSD. Knowing Kevin, he probably would.

The first night I met him, he and Spook tried to break into our local Spar. I had just started seeing their friend, the only one with a car, who was acting as their getaway driver. Their plan was to dismantle the shop's alarm then break in and steal booze and fags. Sounded like a good plan, but it took them ages to pull the alarm off the top of the building and it just wouldn't stop going off. We drove away with the alarm. That's all we had: a huge bloody alarm, covered in everyone's jackets to try to stifle the noise, but nothing worked. Stamping on it, hitting it with bricks, throwing it repeatedly against the ground. Nothing. It still went off, louder than fireworks. We drove around frantically, trying to find a spot where we could try to shut it off somehow, whilst hoping that its battery would eventually run out, but no such luck. Everywhere we went, people looked out of their windows. There was no way Kevin and Spook could return to the shop, or anywhere else in the neighbourhood that night. In the end, the boys chucked it down an alleyway and we abandoned the plan to get drunk for free.

Kevin would often turn up to pick me up in a stolen car. I don't even know why he came for me. Why did he always want company if he didn't care about people? He would get someone else to drive the first car while he hot-wired a second, then a third, until he got everyone mobile. He had a trick of getting the registration plates so dirty that they weren't readable. Besides, he tended to drive them in the middle of the night when the owners were still in bed and hadn't yet noticed their car was gone.

He used his charm to get free fuel too. He would go to a petrol station, invariably manned by a lone female worker, and give them some crap story about how his car had been stolen and he had gone to get it back but the thieves had used up all the petrol and, in his haste, he had come out without his wallet.

He was a lanky, spotty teenager! He was at their forecourt window, in the middle of the night, with no money, driving a car with no petrol cap on it (with no key, he'd have to break the petrol cover off). Yet, amazingly, they believed him and would happily take his name and address and let him fuel up. I used to think that he could have made his fortune if only he had used that ability for genuine business, if he had a mind to. He didn't. A few years later, he was dead. He drove a motorbike into a billboard. I don't know how or why (and it probably wasn't even his bike) but it sounded like a cool way to die. And apt, for him.

People use each other for what they can get. Not everyone. As my brother once pointed out: in life, there are the givers and the takers. You're either one or the other. You're the shitter or the shat upon. I don't like those options.

14. FUTILE AMBITION

I've had too much time to think. I read somewhere once that that's just what humans do, we think. It's supposed to set us apart from other animals – the art of contemplation. I don't know whether cats ponder the meaning of life. They certainly spend enough time lying around.

I saw a bird handler once, giving a demonstration at Blair Drummond Safari Park. He brought out this falcon and the bird was wearing a tight leather hood over its head. The guy explained that it helped to calm the bird by blocking everything out. He said that their brains work so fast because they can see and hear much faster than we can. I had thought there was something wrong with me because I think all the time. I just can't switch it off. It helped me to know that even some birds think faster thoughts than I do. But are their thoughts just linked to what they see and hear? I mean, even if I was wearing a hood, I'd still think. I lie in bed, in the darkness, and sometimes cram a pillow over my head to make it even darker and quieter, but my mind is still churning out all this shit. It never stops.

That's why people drink or take drugs. It's like a mini holiday from your normal self - the brain's equivalent to a weekend away. It's just when you can't face going back home, when you want to keep getting drunk, or out of your head a bit on dope, or up on E or speed or coke or whatever, that it becomes a problem. Well, the fact that coming down, or not being drunk or stoned, makes what you had before seem even worse, is scary sometimes. You get all jumpy and jittery. Why put yourself through that and for what? Just keep drinking or smoking every day. Who wants to live until they're old anyway? I don't want to live to be old enough to be shoved into a home with a load of other drooling pensioners that everyone's forgotten about, with overworked staff having to wipe my arse.

Life is so depressing and that's all you've got to look forward to. You think when you're young that anything's possible and that when you grow up, you're going to be rich, successful and happy, world travel guaranteed; that you're going to leave some lasting legacy of greatness, to be appreciated by generations to come. But the reality is, if you're lucky, you might get a minimum wage job, a council house (after many years of waiting) and a Saturday night out at your local, or staying in, watching X Factor with a partner you hate. Why don't schools tell you that?

It's all a big con, like the Jesus fairytale, the Santa conspiracy and the love lie. Why do the sadistic bastards gleefully ask you what you want to be when you grow up and get you to rhyme off your dreams of being a famous footballer or a pop star, when they know fine well you'll be lucky if you so much as get a job on the checkout at Tesco?

At least now the kids' TV programmes are a bit more realistic. It used to be Superman, Wonder Woman and the Six Million Dollar Man, mixed in with the A-Team and the Kids from Fame. Now it's Postman Pat, Fireman Sam and Bob the Builder. The older ones are still being drip fed the lies that they can all be famous singers or footballers though. Teenagers nowadays act like they will have Paris Hilton's trust fund when it comes to thinking about career choices. No wonder they had to start letting the Eastern Europeans come over and do some of the real work.

Ha, when my life gets turned into a Hollywood film because I'm dead or in jail, I bet they turn me into a man. I had this conversation with someone once (probably a man!) about how it's rare that a film is carried entirely by a woman actor. I argued that Angelina Jolie did Tomb Raider and Salt. That would be funny: my life played out with Angelina Jolie as me. Well they'd better hurry up, she's nearly forty. Most actresses don't work beyond that.

There I go again, I can't let it go – the dream of "being" somebody some day, or of being rich, even though I know it will never happen.

And the internet, that's like a new drug, sucking you in with the promise of some light relief from your crap life, but slowly drains you. Suddenly your house is a mess, you just don't seem to get around to washing the clothes, or taking the rubbish out, and there's piles of dirty dishes and a layer of dust everywhere, because you're too busy checking someone else's status on Facebook.

You must check your emails about fifty times a day, just in case. Just in case, there is something great and exciting that will lift you out of the boredom. But all there is are someone else's photos from a night out: a group of people, drinks in hand, all making some stupid face to the camera. Even on the train into town on nights out, people are taking these photos to put on Facebook. Their whole life is planned in advance to capture something to be put on their wall, just so that someone can tag a name and people can write comments and we can all check them out and be even more depressed at our pathetic lives for doing so. Hang on, wait there till I go and check my emails, it might be a message telling me that my whole life so far is actually a hoax and that I'm really the heir to a billion dollar oil company. Aye, right. But we need to believe that because if we don't, what's left? A Prozac prescription.

Now, I know it's common nowadays for your average town's nightclub to feature a "special guest" from the telly or some ex-boyband member, but the whole idea of that just depresses the life right out of me. What, are we all supposed to stand agape while some guy gets up, next to the DJ, and says, "Hello Wigan!"? I could throw myself off the pier just thinking about it. That just sums up how pathetic our existence is, that we are expected to pay money to gawp at some individual off the telly for a few minutes on a night out. The fact that the management is paying him to travel hundreds of miles to be there, simply emphasises the fact that this is not the sort of place people like him go to. Not the club, or the town, or even the country. Or else he wouldn't be on Hollyoaks or TOWIE. If he was actually from "around here" and would go to such a place for a night out, the rest of the time, he'd be down the park, drinking tonic wine, or smoking dope in his bedroom.

I'm fed up reading about celebrities and seeing them on telly, wearing nice clothes and having a great time. It's like rubbing my face in it. And I'm fed up feeling guilty when Christmas rolls round again and not long after, as soon as the Christmas cards are out the shops, they're swiftly replaced by Easter eggs, like some huge fucking retail conveyor belt. That's exactly what it's like. Not just the belt you put your stuff on to pay for it at the checkout; I mean that some bastard has dreamt up all these rituals, just so that we have no choice but to take part in them. None of it's about being nice to the people you care about, or even about God. They're just devices that retailers have thought up so they have you by the short and curlies and you HAVE to buy stuff you don't want or need.

It's no coincidence that the current, socially accepted image of Santa in the West was created by Coca Cola's marketing department. And have you noticed Halloween now has a specific colour theme – black and orange? That came from the leading global capitalists of the world – America - too.

So, like the churches, they have the monopoly on our rituals, but it's a lot cleverer than that. They are actually linking these buying episodes into the yearly calendar (why do we need this yearly device you might wonder?). They are creating a *pattern* link to the seasons that we don't question. We simply accept that it's winter, so we buy STUFF, for Christmas presents; it's autumn, so we buy Halloween tat and fireworks; it's spring, so we buy chocolate for Easter. On and on it goes with Valentine's Day and Mother's Day and Father's Day… At the root of all these "celebrations", some clever person has once asked, "What can we invent to exploit the mugs and force them to spend?" And we *are* mugs and we do spend because everyone else is doing it. I feel like an idiot.

I don't have any money. It sickens me, being forced to try and buy stuff when it's hard enough just to heat the house and buy food. I got fed up with having to go to bed during the day, dressed, just to keep warm. Of course, there is always someone worse off and I'm not heartless. I see those pictures of starving kids in other countries and feel terrible for them but it's not MY fault. But somebody out there is taking everything, while the rest of us have nothing.

I might be lucky to have more than people in East Timor and I'm warmer than people in Russia, but I still don't have an easy or a good time. That's why people buy Lottery tickets and lap up stuff like The Secret. They want a better life. But they are <u>never</u> going to get it. They can place as many cosmic orders out of their windows to the stars at night as they like, but they'll still be working for the council, emptying the bins until they retire (if they're lucky).

I'm not a total moron. I don't just wish and dream about things. I haven't got one of those visualisation boards. I don't sit about, cutting out pictures of the things I want. I don't download the schedule on the million pound mansion house I'd love to own, or ask to test drive a Jaguar XK8 at my local car showroom. Who actually believes THAT? Millions of people. Rhonda Byrne's certainly lived well off of it.

I did consider it. I was almost sucked in. I mean, wouldn't it be great? But it's also like the time I almost bought an ab trainer from Amazon that promised to give you a "six pack in six weeks" if you used the trainer for just ten minutes a day. Until I realised that you also had to be the right weight in the first place, eat healthily and also do regular exercise (in that case, you wouldn't need to fork out for an ab trainer machine).

But I can understand why people need to fall for all this new worldy stuff and neuro-linguistic programming rubbish. You only have to think about something and it's yours. Really.

15. POWERLESS

My dad had been such a formidable and strong man. When we ran home from school, he would be sitting in his arm chair by the coal fire, glass of lager in hand, with another four or five cans of Breaker warming on the hearth.

He drove the bingo buses at his work with cans of Breaker down the side of his driver's seat. All the old women would tell us what a terrible driver he was and moan when he cornered too fast or hit bumps on the road.

At weekends, he drank more. Usually some wine with his dinner and Bacardi if he wanted to get really drunk. When he was at home, he sat in his chair at one end of the long, narrow living room, watching the telly at the other end, so that our living room was often in complete darkness, except from the flickering flames of the fire and the glow of the TV. We weren't allowed to talk or move from the couch if we wanted to sit in there. There was no central heating or double glazing in those days, so that was the only warm room in the house. We had a choice of sitting in silence, in the dark, watching Steve Davis play snooker, or going up to our freezing rooms with no TV, no music, no computer and no books. It was quite a miserable life, but it forced us to spend a lot of time outdoors or using our imaginations. But maybe that's where I learned to think too much and too darkly.

Gradually, the bingo hall started to get competition from the bigger national companies like Mecca and Gala, until it was forced to close down. My dad was made redundant. He became very depressed and the structure went out of his days. He began drinking more and more. It was a terrible time at home. My parents suddenly had no escape from each other and half the money they'd been used to was gone, so they were arguing constantly. We had school then when we got in, sitting in silence as my dad watched TV and drank and my mum worked constant backshift. When they were home together at weekends, they argued, sometimes violently. With my dad now at home constantly, including school holidays, our already miserable lives were even worse.

They eventually split up, but not until my brothers and I were all in our late teens. My dad ended up alone in a flat. For a time, he managed to get another job but by then, his drinking was so out of control that he needed to drink as soon as he woke up just to stop the shakes and to "top up" throughout the day, just to function normally. So he was soon sacked from the new job and confined himself to the bedroom of his flat where he drank all day, every day.

It got to the stage where his body could no longer tolerate food, only alcohol. I tried to help him, cleaned up his flat, took him food, bought him clothes and a mobile phone. At times, he would want to stop drinking and get help, but the "help" never came.

One of the doctors at my dad's practice spoke to me in a condescending tone and said that he knew I "wanted to help" and called me "dear", but refused to give my dad anything except thiamine tablets, saying that there was little point trying to detox him because he would just go straight back to drinking and that he would be dead from an infection in a few weeks anyway.

His flat was rancid. As soon as you got near the block, even from outside, you could smell his house, like a low, steady noxious hum. He would crawl to the door, naked, to let me in (before he finally gave me a key).

He was too weak to walk or dress himself in the months before he died. He was doubly incontinent – or at least too weak to get to the toilet, and urinated in coke bottles, which gathered around his bed and his diarrhoea stained a trail along the hall carpet and walls but stopped short of the bathroom, because he never managed to drag himself to the toilet in time.

The place was thick with huge, buzzing bluebottles. You just can't capture that level of filth by describing it. I don't think it would even work if you tried to film it. Even photographs of the actual piles of rotting rubbish don't attack your senses and make you feel sick the way the thick, putrid air of stale urine, vomit and excrement can. Nor do pictures make you shudder in the same way as the sight of live, wriggling maggots in food cartons and fully-grown flies buzzing around your ears as soon as you walk through the door.

I think he used a 'dial-a-drink' service to bring him the coke, vodka and cigarettes. He was losing touch with reality and was convinced his neighbours were plotting against him. They probably were though. I wouldn't have wanted to live anywhere near him. Many times, I tried to persuade him to go to hospital, but he kept refusing. He had always hated hospitals, being convinced that if you went there, you would surely die. But more than that, I don't think he realised how bad he was. That's the thing with alcoholics, they get so used to lying to themselves that they've got everything under control, that no matter how bad they get, how close to death they are, they think they're fine. They're like the opposite of hypochondriacs.

I would stand at the bottom of his bed, tears rolling down my cheeks, and ask him just to stop drinking. I had no idea then that it can be fatal for an alcohol dependant person to suddenly stop drinking. I didn't realise that he needed a medical detox. I didn't understand the horrors of withdrawal that he must have faced as soon as he woke up in the morning and would get worse until he raised that first drink of the day to his lips – the sweats, the tremors, the feeling as though your skin is crawling, anxiety, hallucinations. It's supposed to be worse than cold turkey from heroin. An addicted person feels literally as though they are dying, if they don't get their next hit or drink. People end up so bad that they can't go without it at all. In the end, they need to drink constantly, even through the night, just to keep the horrendous withdrawal symptoms at bay. It must be exhausting.

I became like the parent of this pathetic, grotesque child that I had to visit in a filthy, fly-infested hovel and yet I was totally unable to change anything. I felt powerless. My formidable oppressor and protector in one had become dependent on me, yet I could do nothing to help. I couldn't even bring him to live with me in his last dying days because I was registered homeless, sleeping on the floor of a freezing flat in a nearby town with my children after splitting with my husband. He was too thin to travel and he would not have survived in my cold flat. Even if I had cleaned his flat again (as I had many times), it was too small for me and the children. Everything was so bleak.

I managed to get him to the hospital in the end, so that at least he died in a clean bed, where, in that sanitised environment, draped in white sheets, his family could all pay their last respects and say, "Goodbye".

Despite everything, he still had some pride. It amazes me how alcoholics can do that. No matter how bad their life, they will still cling on to a tiny scrap that represents the boundary of their self-esteem. They might have let almost everything else in their life go: their home, their job, their relationships, their personal hygiene, but there will still be something that they will cling on to, perhaps all part of that ruse to themselves that they are still in control and are okay.

Patricia once insisted on putting on lipstick before she went to hospital, regardless of the fact that she had barely washed in days, had spent her days lying around in bed, naked, because of the sweats (and oblivious to the needs of her family), and had barely eaten for weeks. How inspiringly tragic, that last chink of pride, in human nature, in the face of death from addiction.

Telling me to go home, that he didn't want us to see him being sick in the hospital, was the last time my dad ever spoke to me. If I had known that was my last conversation with him, would I have made it count?

I hardly see my mother these days. Sometimes, I drive past her house and think about her inside. I feel guilty for driving past, in a hurry as usual to go somewhere, get something done and then torture myself, imagining what it will be like when she's dead and I no longer have the chance to pop in and see her. Would I long to see her again and wish I had spent more time phoning her, visiting her, taking more of an interest? Will I suddenly be able to recall, in great detail, every good deed she has done for me since early childhood? What if she doesn't die quickly, but lingers slowly on, becoming totally dependent on me first? Will I resent her being a burden? I am aware of the possibility that she might die any time, or more realistically, that she's not getting any younger, so it will be at least some time in the next few years. But nothing makes me take the opportunity I have now to see her and spend time with her, while she is still physically and mentally independent. Why?

At times, I think that there is something lacking in me, that I can go through life and not admit the most obvious of things to myself: that the frailty of the human existence, as reflected in my parents' mortality (if not my own) scares me. It scares me so much that I run and hide from it and avoid it at all costs. My mother could be lying in front of me now, with a steak knife in her chest, gurgling her last, bloody breaths and I would frantically – but somehow in a calm and detached way – be telling myself that she was fine, that she'll be around forever. And, when I have more time, I'll see her…

16. USELESS

AA tells people to "make a moral inventory" of themselves. Not the Automobile Association, obviously. Well my advice to you is: never try to make an inventory of yourself, moral or otherwise. You might think that you have a lot to say and that you have a great personality, but if you really think about it, turn yourself over, there might not be much there. You'll be left disappointed, short-changed, and realising you're not as great as you thought you were. Especially, don't do it just before coming up to a mid-life event like your fortieth birthday, or later, when you retire. There's even less time then to become that "urbane, windswept and interesting fellow" that Billy Connolly used to joke about in his stand-up routine. More likely, you will realise the truism of the advice I was given once, just after being sacked:

"You have a very high opinion of yourself. Unfortunately, that's not a view shared by other people."

I loved that. Classic. Not only have we told you to fuck off because you were crap at your job, but you are fucking useless in general. You might as well kill yourself now. I had to laugh. They all hated each other in that office and didn't have time to lift their heads up from their work for two minutes, yet still worked twelve hours a day and at weekends – with no overtime payments - just to keep up with their workloads. They rarely had a lunch-break. If they were really lucky and feeling quite blasé, they might be able to squeeze in the odd ten minutes at the tan stand across the road from the office, to jiggle about on a vibration plate. I had been given a "get out of jail free" card.

What is employment anyway? You work for money in order to buy things. But you are not trading your work fairly for the work of other human beings in the world – the things you buy. But they are not the only ones being exploited. A large portion of the money you work for is taken by the government as tax, which it uses to pay off the national debt, or the interest on it. We are *indebted*. We can't opt out of this system. It's enslavement.

Even if I bought a bit of land and decided to simply live off it and collect rain water, I would still have to pay some form of tax, at the very least, Council Tax. So, if I was living off my own land, just staying there, going nowhere else, I would still need to raise money to pay the government to pay off the debt it has accrued with someone else. So, I'm a slave. And have my children, grandchildren and great grandchildren (not yet born) already been sold into this same slavery? It applies to all of us. Yet we don't even know who we are enslaved to. Do you know who your government owes money to? How much, and for how long? What terms did they agree? Was the debt written with your name on it?

17. INEQUALITY

A few things got me started questioning this state of affairs. The first was the realisation that I would always be poor and get nowhere, while some people out there were very, very wealthy. Then it was reading Chuck Palahniuk's Fight Club and a visit from a couple of Mormons.

I agreed with Nietzsche's philosophy, but it's hardly a blueprint for success for someone like me: living your life the way you are supposed to, being the best that you can be and acting altogether as if you're following a universal law. That isn't easy. I loved Palahniuk's idea of revenge against the big businesses. But I disagreed with him on the materialism. He saw people as enslaved by their things. I understand that. But there's an underclass of people who can still only aspire to having something out of an IKEA catalogue. Maybe it does make you free, only having what you need. Buying your furniture and clothes second-hand from charity shops and car boot sales seems like the *right* thing to do because it's more sustainable. It bucks the trend of keeping up with the Joneses; it is recycling and it doesn't support our capitalist, materialistic culture. For all those reasons, I agree that buying used goods is a worthy thing to do. But it doesn't feel so good having second-hand stuff, if you don't have a choice.

If you are stuck in the same society as everyone else, but you are at the bottom of the pile – the wrong class, in a town, in a country, where generations and generations before you have worked as little more than slaves and nothing has changed, that's not some sort of hippy choice to opt out. More like, that's a case of not being allowed to have the things everyone else takes for granted. That pisses me off. I wear second-hand clothes and my house is full of second-hand furniture, but not because I have decided that's what I *want* but because that's all I can afford. But I don't sit and waste time thinking about why I can't have stuff from IKEA. I think about why I can't have a huge palace, or why other people do and I don't.

So I just didn't get why Palahniuk's narrator character would give up a pristine flat and all his stuff and that good lifestyle for squatting. Well, I liked that he squatted in a mansion, but I just think he should have done it up, or taken over a less dilapidated stately home and got a few luxuries. What was Tyler Durden fed up with? Being a corporate slave? Being emasculated? Well I'm fed up with having no money and no prospects in a world that is totally unfair. We sit and we moan that someone from another country comes here and gets a house, or claims benefits and insist that "everyone should be made to work". Why? So that the richest 1% of the population can add to their billions?

And those Mormons. Two eager and serene boys who stood on my doorstep one night, dressed in suits, who spoke about their religion that they had obviously lapped up, literally, as the world's salvation solution and, like enthusiastic puppies, now ran around neighbourhoods, wagging with excitement, spreading the word to save old cynics like me. They are adoring, unquestioning followers, out trying to recruits others, just like the Jehovahs or the Krishnas.

Those boys could have just been a sexual fantasy of mine later (yes, women do that too), but something in the way they dutifully and solemnly told me all about their church and left me with a pamphlet and a bible (which they seemed overjoyed about, even though they gave me it for free), left me touched. I even considered for a minute whether to go to their church until I read in the pamphlet that when attending services the "ladies usually wore dresses, or skirts and blouses" and realised that I'd never fit in with my usual uniform of jeans and boots. And the feminist in me raged that I would be expected to conform to some male-imposed, demure, girly dress code.

But the point is, these young guys were giving up their free time to try to recruit people. They actually believed in what they had been told and were out, trying to spread the word. I loved that.

I read about their bible and how this guy, Joseph Smith, founded their religion and I thought, "I could do that". The idea of having that power, having young guys like that go out and do things for me, was seductive. For the first time in ages, I had a feeling that I could do something. People needed a leader. They needed someone who knew what it was like to have been fucked over by the rich upper and middle classes who ran the world, leaving the rest of us with nothing but cheap booze, Facebook and the X Factor to make our lives bearable. But these things don't really make our lives tolerable, they just distract us.

Everyone around me had gone to the dogs or died. I had been sacked. I had no money. I was bored. I needed a direction. I wanted to do something with my life. Not doing anything, passively accepting my fate, had left me depressed. I wanted to believe in individual responsibility, that we are all in charge of our own destiny and that there are no external factors to stop us achieving our aims, but it was so difficult to know *what* to do. And what about the lack of resources?

18. THE ENEMY

How can you target your enemy? The trouble is, I've never been that interested in politics. It's difficult to imagine who to vent your anger at when you don't know who to be annoyed at. So I Googled "Who Owns the World" and found a list of land owners, topped by the Queen. I then looked up the 'Forbes Rich List' and found the world's top billionaires. It also lists where they got their money from, such as Wal-Mart, L'Oreal and H&M. That then led me to looking up stuff about secret societies, Zionists, Freemasons, the Illuminati and the Annunaki but, by then, I didn't know what to believe.

There was a lot of stuff written about the world's richest family, the Rothschilds. Why aren't they called

Rothschildren? I don't understand why they're not top of the Forbes List. Maybe they don't declare their assets, or maybe their massive fortune is split up amongst their large family so that none of them, individually, appear to be the richest person in the world.

The Rothschilds are supposed to have funded some of the world's richest families, such as Carnegie and Rockefeller (I'm not sure where I read that). Imagine a family being so rich that it could afford to lend money to those two (and many others). If that's true, that is wealth beyond most ordinary people's imagination. There are so many conspiracy theories about whether they have financed wars, royal families and governments, and about how they own the world's media. The stuff written about them seems pretty damning, if they really do have that much money in that one family, whilst millions die of starvation – enough money to totally eradicate world poverty. How could I be sure any of it was true? But the idea held at least the possibility of a grain of truth: somebody somewhere must be the source of the world's wealth. If it's not all these governments whose economies are collapsing all around us under mountains of debt, then it must be someone even richer than them that they owe all this debt to. So it does not really matter which political party is in office. Even they cannot do anything about the debt their country already owes.

There was also a lot of controversy about the secret meetings of the Bilderberg Group of international power brokers. There are theories about how this select group of people - not the world's governments – meet up to decide how the world will be run.

Obviously, now that the group is known about, it will have to change its identity and meet up somewhere else, so that it can continue its secret management of the globe without scrutiny. But is this true? Could one family be richer than governments and they and their associates be running the whole world? I didn't know what to believe. It certainly has the ingredients of a great conspiracy theory. The one thing I do think though, is that where there's money, there's power.

Of course there's nothing official to prove this theory, well none that I had the time to look in to, so it's all just hypothesis. I'll re-cap what I've said, although bear in mind that I don't know anything for sure. All I've figured out is that, contrary to what we have been taught to believe, governments might not be ruling the world: those with the most money are. That at least includes the über rich Rothschilds and much "smaller fry" like Warren Buffet and the Waltons who own Wal-Mart. (Tesco is owned by shareholders, I checked that too.)

Anyway, amongst other things, the people who rule the world get their money from the things they sell, so any products or services that we spend money on makes them richer and the rest of us poorer. Simple.

So when you realise that the multinational companies who provide goods and services are owned by the ones in the world who have all the money and the power, those companies could easily become the natural targets for your frustration. Chuck Palahniuk got it right in Fight Club with his Project Mayhem. I wouldn't want to achieve anarchy or chaos though. I hate the thought of people getting hurt or being killed. I don't watch

TV and try not to read the news, but I still managed to catch a glimpse of a gruesome picture of a young guy who'd had both his legs blown off in the Boston marathon. It was horrific and senseless. Rationally, I can appreciate that such attacks are easier to carry out and get a lot of publicity, but even if I was hell-bent on destruction and killing (which I never could be), I wouldn't want to hurt or kill innocent bystanders. If you're determined to make a stand, shouldn't you aim for the actual people you're angry with?

I just wish that the rich weren't so smug. It would be great, I think, if they could worry about the fact that we are out here, by the millions, in these deprived areas, seemingly quiet and unquestioning for now, but in actual fact, we are seething with a hatred for them and their wealth that the odd act of criminal damage will not satisfy.

I've got no master plan with a utopian ideal of stripping the Rothschild family and their friends of all their wealth and redistributing it fairly around the world so that every person had the right to basic things like food, water, shelter and freedom (although of course that would be great). No, I'm not that idealistic. I'm just pissed off at being poor myself with few prospects.

It's hard to keep a positive attitude when no matter what you seem to do, nothing changes. You are bombarded with messages from every corner – billboards, TV, internet, radio, catalogues, window displays - that you should have this and have done that. It makes you feel cheated when you don't have any of it.

I sometimes feel as though I'm outside the rest of the world, just looking in. I suppose that's what "disenfranchised" means. You realise that it's all just a big con. None of those things were *ever* meant for you. You're never going to get them. Things are just dangled in front of you, like a carrot and you're the stupid donkey, the beast of burden, carrying everything on its back and trudging the same worn out path your parents did and their parents before them.

19. THE UNDERCLASS

People from the middle and upper classes probably think the lower class – certainly the underclass - are frightening, distasteful, a scourge on society, and that we're basically a bunch of scroungers who don't even try to help ourselves. Historians like Welshman and even psychiatrists like Theodore Dalrymple have written about Britain's "underclass", but they write from an outsider's perspective, lacking empathy and realism. They think they know the underclass, but they don't. Even I don't fully know what it's like to be part of the underclass, because although I live in it, I'm still a bit more "fortunate" (or at least different), because I've had a higher education and I'm more resourceful by nature than most of my peers seem to be.

But people like Dalrymple don't even come close to understanding what it is like to be at the bottom of the pile. They are middle class, well-educated and have well-paying careers. Their parents and grandparents were probably middle class too.

Lately, we've had MPs coming away with how they could easily live on £12.80 a week for their food shopping. That's true. You could. But would you *want* to, day in, day out, year after year, with just the basics to eat? Even that would be doable, especially if you lived in a really poor country where everyone else was scraping by on the same amount, but imagine you lived in a rich country, where you were bombarded constantly with images of things you don't have. Then it's two years down the line and you still have no job; you badly need a haircut; your children need shoes;

Christmas is coming up; they need new coats; your washing machine has broken down and one of your kids has been invited to a friend's birthday party…the list goes on and on.

Those MPs and the other opinionated inhumanitarians like Dalrymple don't know what it's like to have been born into a deprived town, where generation after generation of your friends and relatives have nothing, even though they work out in all weathers on freezing concrete under cars, in fish factories, or cleaning out toilets (if they are the lucky ones with jobs).

They don't know what it's like to stand in a queue in the corner shop, where everyone in front of them is buying fags and bottles of tonic wine or vodka because they've bought into the myth that this is the only way to make life more bearable – a way that they are blamed for and which will ultimately cost them their lives. Or to live in a street controlled by a CCTV camera that never seems to capture the fights, or the stones being thrown at your windows, or the teenagers stealing plastic wheelie bins, or those kids setting the bins on fire to inhale the fumes because they've been told it gets you high. Their teenagers won't be sitting outside in the freezing cold next to a wheelie bin ablaze, inhaling toxic fumes for a hit.

They don't have to lie awake worrying at night about paying their gas and electricity bills, while their kids lie awake and worry that they don't have the right high street brand labels to wear. They're not single parents who are worn out with the daily grind of caring for children, in a "no-frills" lifestyle and arguing with the drug addict ex-partner. Neither did they ever experience the buzz when they were young, of running about with all their mates, feeling invincible, because they've intimidated a rival gang with bricks and broken bottles then sat around, laughing about it, over a joint. They haven't experienced the grief of a friend dying on the cusp of manhood because he got so drunk at the park that he fell in the river and drowned. They haven't thought they were dying all day on a Sunday, because they've gone over the score and taken too much speed or ten Es and danced all night at The Arches to heavy house, played so loud you can feel it vibrating through your bones. They haven't lived an underclass life.

"Working class" only applies if you actually have a job, no matter how crappy that job. And the working class and the "non-working" underclass live in the same streets, as neighbours. There is no real difference then to their culture, so when people (usually middle class people) talk about the underclass or the working class, they are talking about people who live in the same environment, side-by-side, as neighbours. But the ruling classes aren't stupid: they know that fine well. That's why they push this idea in the media they own, of "benefit thieves", aiming it at the working class with low paid jobs. They know that some people in that environment will work most of their lives, whereas others will be without a job. They know the ones that work (and the ones that don't or can't) will be unhappy with what little they've got.

Cleverly, they drip feed them lies about how those on benefits are "stealing" from the ones with the crappy jobs. They do this to set them against each other like two starving bull terriers in a fighting pit, the poor dogs tearing each other to pieces to survive while the organisers make money from them. While the lower classes (working and non-working) are busy fighting amongst each other and blaming those around them for their impoverished situation, they are distracted from the fact that someone else is sitting there, in billions of pounds' worth of luxury, laughing their heads off at the stupidity of everyone else.

Children don't ask for their parents to be on benefits and people don't want to get old or be too young and inexperienced for work. And those who have never worked, like their parents before them, don't have the self-esteem that comes with being productive and having the routine of work. We shouldn't be angry with them.

People like Dalrymple seem to actually think it's just a lack of personal responsibility that makes an underclass, or some kind of liberal social engineering project gone wrong: that people don't do enough for themselves; that they expect things to be handed to them. Even if it was that simple, why not? Isn't that the price that should be paid for silence? Other people have argued that the reason that England pays a block grant to Scotland and Northern Ireland under the Barnett Formula is to buy their (mute) dependence.

Like their dependent nations, the underclass has been trained to be powerless, unquestioning and basically, unenterprising. To be anything other would require skills and knowledge that might make such people question a state of affairs that, even if they do work all of their lives, they will still have a very poor lifestyle – nothing - compared with the middle and upper classes, who have generations upon generations of an inheritable head start that the lower classes will NEVER catch up with.

It's only now that the middle classes are starting to murmur, because their inheritance is also being taken away – on nursing fees for their elderly parents, and more recently, because of the fact that they now can't afford to finance their children through university.

All of a sudden, the English middle classes aren't so smug. But they still look to the other countries, especially Scotland, and think it's *their* fault ("but Scotland's pensioners get free nursing care" and "Scotland's university students get their fees paid"). Don't they realise that swathes of Scottish people have lived in huge sink estates of council houses for generations and there just isn't a house to sell? And the Scottish students can all go to university and get as many qualifications as they like, but they still won't get a good job. There are far fewer graduate-calibre jobs here. But the real point is that it's not the devolved countries' faults that these English people are having to pay nursing fees and for university tuition; it's the government's. And the government owes all that money out (to whom?).

People need to think about tracing along to who is actually stealing their inheritance. If they did, they would soon find out it's not their neighbours in Britain, or people seeking asylum in the UK, or even the great unwashed who spend their lives on the dole. It's the people with so many sumptuous buildings, grander than any royal palaces. They have so many, in fact, that they have given dozens of their huge buildings away for free, to charity (how big of them), whilst the Englishman's family home, his "castle", is sold off and the proceeds taken by the State to pay its debts. At least you had that nice home for a little while. We didn't.

20. PROFIT & PRINCIPLES

I think in order to get on in life, to make lots of money, you have to be unscrupulous. You have to not care about whether other people suffer and die because of your need for money. That might sound a bit histrionic, but I could not have been the successful proprietor of, say, a tobacco company, paying the poor tobacco growers a pittance for their crop, and as little as they possibly can to whoever rolls it into paper to make the cigarettes and boxes them up for sale. I don't imagine those factory workers are well looked after. Then there's the finished product itself, it contains proven carcinogens. As a way of making vast amounts of money, getting people addicted to something that you pay as little as possible to produce, is genius. But could you

sell a product that you know harms people? The tobacco industry has.
I would be no good as the owner of a pharmaceutical company either. I would want a cure to be found for the world's diseases and to genuinely treat the sick, not work out ways of producing medicines so that cures were not a priority, but long term "management" of illness was, so that countries had to keep on buying my products to treat people. I wouldn't consider enforcing the patent on my medicines against the world's poorest countries so that they had to pay over the odds for my brand, even where a cheaper generic drug might allow them to save lives. How could anyone deprive sick people, especially in developing countries, of vital medicine? The pharmaceutical industry has.

If you think about it, long-term illnesses, for which no cure has been found, are the perfect scenario for the owners of drug companies. If they could cure cancer completely with a single pill – would they? I doubt it, because they would lose billions of pounds in chemo and radiotherapies and pain relief. It's the same with HIV. AIDS hasn't been cured, but – great news for those billionaires who own the companies that produce these drugs – people living with HIV can now live for the rest of their lives (a normal lifespan) on medication.

Mental illness is just the same: you can live a normal life with a mental illness, *as long as* you keep taking anti-depressants for years, often for the rest of your life. Who benefits from the millions of people in developed countries who are on anti-depressants? The owners of drug companies of course.

And consider this, why are people in developing countries not more depressed than we are? Oh, it's not that they're not depressed. Is it that they just can't afford Prozac? And then there's the more obvious point that they are too busy with trying to find clean water and enough to eat (basic survival) to stop and consider how they might feel about it.

I couldn't take coffee and bananas from poor third world growers for a pittance, make someone else out there transport it for me for a paltry sum too and then sell those things for a huge profit in shops in richer countries. I live in the West, on a very low income, and yet I can't bring myself to buy the cheapest Smartprice bananas because I feel so guilty about it. I opt for Fairtrade every time. Yet it isn't me who's profiting from these poor farmers.

I used to feel guilty about going into Primark, because they were selling clothes so cheaply that they couldn't possibly have paid a fair price for all the materials and workmanship that went into making them (and there might have been a bit of a brand backlash over how ethical Primark's trading policy was), but now the charity shops are charging more for second hand Primark brands than they cost new. So what choice does this give to someone who is being priced out of charity shops now?

I think charity shops should bear in mind that they have a duty to provide for the poor in the town they retail in first of all. Quite a few managers of these shops seem to think we all usually shop at M&S and only come into a charity shop now and then for the odd knitting pattern, hardback autobiography of Gloria Hunniford, and some charity

Christmas cards. Some of us actually need to buy our clothes there.

I couldn't manufacture chocolate using child labour. I couldn't sell infant formula milk to mothers of babies in countries where there is no clean water supply, so that their own breast milk dries up and their babies die because there is no clean water to make up formula milk. I could not almost drain a country's water supply to fulfil the demands for my carbonated drink around the world. Global companies have done all of these things.

I could not keep animals in cages so tiny that they cannot move and have to live in their own filth, and have to be pumped full of antibiotics in order to survive long enough to be fattened up for slaughter, and then kill those animals for money. Nor could I take away their calves as soon as they are born in order to keep the mother cows going as milk machines to maximise my profits. I'm a vegetarian who, in all consciousness, should not be drinking cows' milk either.

I wouldn't pillage the sea of all her fish, taking what I would get most profit from under my quota and then chuck the rest back, dead. Nor do I think it's right that food is bought from poor countries then shipped around the world, just so that we can eat fruits and vegetables out of season.

I could not make people work long hours in hot factories to make products or clothes for me to sell. Even if I owned an office-based business in the UK, I would want to pay my workers well above the average wage, let them work flexitime, have generous holidays, paid lunch breaks and would hope that they enjoyed their work. Clearly, I am far too sentimental and principled to be successful in business.

21. PROTEST

So here I am, with this awful feeling of isolation. I had hoped in my youth that this sense of alienation was a teenage thing, something that I would mature out of (once I grew up a bit and "became part of society"). But I think the sense that you're on your own only intensifies with age. It has for me. I clearly have this bitterness about how my life has ended up as opposed to how it ought to be, but I'm now beginning to wonder who decides how I "ought" to be?

I'm actually content not being too materialistic, if I'm honest with myself. The things that make me happiest are free: the changing of the seasons and the beauty of nature. I can feel over-awed just by being surrounded by trees; or seeing the sun shining over an expanse of water; or marvelling at tiny shoots peeping from the soil; or waking up to find the world around me covered in snow; or looking up and delighting in the sky being so clear that I can make out hundreds of stars and fill my lungs deeply with fresh clean air; or smell the freshness of the grass and see the steam rise up from wood as the morning gets warmer; or see the birds hop and bob for food... but even that quiet reverie is broken into by the thought that a large part of my favourite country park – one of the great pleasures left in my life - has just been fenced off, with the warning that it is protected by some security firm and 24-hour CCTV.

All those trees will be hacked down because somebody else, somewhere else, has decided that the land would be "better" used for something else. No doubt something that will bring in a profit. That makes me white with fury.

But I think protest is a waste of time. Besides, I don't live anywhere near parliament, even the Scottish parliament is miles away. There are no huge centres of governance anywhere around here. That's probably quite deliberate. No, in fact, no politician is poor enough to live around here. I think the nearest place of protest might be the civic centre in the next town, but that's staffed by idiotic local councillors and mainly used for musicals and pantomimes. How apt, now I think about its dual use.

It makes me think that the reason we don't know who is actually running the world is so that we don't protest, or rise up in revolt against them. They are not a target if they are not identifiable. Their power – and therefore the outrage against them and the blame for the world's state of affairs – is diluted and distributed out to heads of nation states (political and royal figureheads), then further dispersed to devolved and local governments in an intricate web of subterfuge.

There is no way the local council here would stop the work on the park that it has already decided on, approved, and has underway. Local people's views are not listened to. The work will go ahead regardless of what the tax payers want. "Tax Payers" – ha, that phrase is bandied about as though that gives rights instead of a burden to pay tax; as though it somehow gives a voice in political affairs. From now on, for "Tax Payers", read, "Slaves".

Even though I don't expect to get anywhere in politics, local or national, I considered some kind of indirect protest against businesses, like organising a "don't buy anything day", or "don't drink cola", or "don't use your car for a week", but quickly realised it wouldn't work. People don't get excited about being told what not to do and they won't put themselves to any inconvenience. It is only when they get inconvenienced, especially with road works, that they really seem to get riled, but not enough to take any direct action.

On YouTube, someone posted a video of an eggshell disintegrating in a glass of cola, warning people not to drink fizzy drinks because it will ruin their teeth and bones. Some of the comments in response were quite vicious by people basically saying, "Don't tell me not to have something I enjoy". Like smoking or drinking, people know the dangers now, but they're still not prepared to give up. So no-one is going to deprive themselves of anything for a day, let alone a week, just to protest against big businesses.

A mobile phone mast was scheduled in this town, for outside a primary school. There was a letter in the local paper, but that's it. No protest. Parents turn up to drop their children off at the school's fancy dress Halloween party by the car load, and will gather around the school gates every day, chatting to their pals for hours, but they won't bother their arses protesting against a potentially harmful mast right next to their children's school. I mean, how hard would it be to hold up a few homemade placards, while they talk about what was on telly last night?

I can't talk. I wouldn't bother protesting either. There's no point.

There is no such thing as democracy.

Think about it. How do you protest against "The System" when:

1. you're not too sure who or what you're protesting against;
2. you don't actually believe in protesting (because done legitimately, it's futile);
3. you don't want the repercussions of breaking the law; and
4. you are the kind of person who writes lists?

So you can probably get the idea – as it started to dawn on me – how impotent we actually are (well, I am). How imprisoned. We are unhappy, but what can we actually do about it? Nothing. When you realise that, you're fucked.

22. ACTION

If anything is going to capture people's interest, it has to be action, especially doing something they're not supposed to. We've all still got a rebellious child in us somewhere. Or maybe that's just me. But maybe other people's hidden children still like to create a bit of havoc. That's what you have to tap into. Or, at the very least, let them have a photo they can put on a social networking site.

All those internet crazes – planking, owling, teapotting, tombstoning and headless horsemanning – they all have these things in common. What they lack though (and no-one cares about this bit) is any sense of purpose. Their sole point is material for Facebook, and perhaps a bit of kudos for the poster. Their fifteen seconds of fame or pride as they bask in the reflection of 193 "Likes".

23. CULT LEADERSHIP

I loved the idea of being a cult leader, but I told myself that it was highly unlikely. I mean, I'm more Adrian Mole than David Koresh. Besides, I knew people would expect me to be a man. It's irritating, but society is still so sexist.

That said though, I'm sure there are plenty of submissive men out there, who secretly love to be bossed around. I reckoned I would have no trouble recruiting men if I wore a pencil skirt and high heels. Men love that saucy secretary look. Shit, I'd be no good as a radical feminist with talk like that. But who cares? Men of the world, follow me (in my stilettos) and if you're really good boys, I might walk all over you in my heels later, while I humiliate your efforts to please me.

If I was applying for the job, and the application form asked me what skills/attributes I'd bring to the post, I'd write something like:

I've got what it takes to be a cult leader. I have a strong, controlling and manipulative personality. I like submissive people. The idea of having power over others excites me. I enjoy telling other people how to dress, what relationships they can have, what job they can do, what possessions they can keep, how they can spend their spare time and their money. In fact, I like controlling every aspect of another person's life – basically how to think, act and speak – that comes naturally to me. Just ask my ex-husband.

As a cult leader, you have to take total control over your members' time and activities and expect complete obedience to you. It's a full-time job. Not so good if you value your own personal space. You have to constantly keep your followers busy in activities that will physically and emotionally drain them, so that they have no time left for any privacy or self-reflection. Otherwise, they could question your authority. The easiest way of doing this is to keep people in groups and to make them do everything together. That means living together, 24/7, with no private space, just doing everything as one unit. That's the simplest method to get your average cult going.

But that would drive me to distraction. I mean, even children go out to play. It's bad enough being cooped up with them at weekends, on a rainy day. Imagine having to live your adult life in a commune? I'm with Sartre on this one: hell is other people.

Imagine being responsible for a group of adults, not normal adults, but a bunch of exceptionally needy adults, who'd follow you around, hanging onto your every word, like Brian Cohen's followers in Monty Python's Life of Brian.

You also have to be willing to shame and humiliate people within the group. Play them off against each other, get a bit of competitiveness going, and get them to vie for your affection and praise. One of the best ways of getting individual members to worship you is just to praise a single person and really build them up for a week or two. It makes the others jealous and gets that person – the pet – dependent on the praise. They get to the point where they need it.

Now I realise my parents used these mind control tactics for years.

Most people who join a cult are really just seeking a bit of praise and affection. Give them that for a week or two, lull them into a false sense of security, then you take it away again, slowly. So that next, you go the other way and start to criticise the person. Just a nasty comment, here or there, or a sign of disappointment with a tut now and then, until you chip away at their self-esteem, bit-by-bit. They will do ANYTHING then to get back in your favour because they'll have become addicted to pleasing you. It's that age-old fear of rejection. In fact, many cult characteristics are the same as parenting techniques. I should maybe write a handbook for any future would-be cult leaders. Look out for it.

Then you can start on someone else in your group. It's a rolling process. Soon, they will all be fighting like starlings over a handful of crumbs for a special look or a compliment, even a bit of criticism gives them that tiny bit of attention they crave.

Clearly, you can't allow people to question your leadership in a cult. Any questions must be deflected back to the questioner as someone who is a mistrustful outsider, who in turn has to be viewed with suspicion by everyone else.

Getting people to reveal their innermost secrets to you as cult leader, or to the whole group, is a handy ploy. You can use it to make people feel forgiven and accepted, bonding them to the group and you can also use it to blackmail them later, should they ever try to leave.

And the advantage of being a cult leader is that you can do what you like. Even if you are an ugly old guy who has an aversion to washing and shaving, you still get your pick of nubile young women to have sex with, whenever and wherever you want. I loved that idea. Imagine me, leading a cult of fit young men. "You and you, come with me for your initiation ceremony. The rest of you, cleanse the clothes and dishes of the group and prepare a celebration feast for later." (Basically, do the washing and dishes and get the dinner on, while I have sex with these two young studs.)

Of course, there would have to be a focus on a perceived enemy – the über rich and their corporations and brands, in this case - to keep the followers busy. As for recruiting people, it's much like religion and relationships. It's easiest to get people to join when they are at their most vulnerable emotionally, especially after someone close to them dies, but also when they are just new to the area, or have just been dumped or made redundant, or if they are young and lonely. Then you welcome them in and seem really friendly and loving, make them feel special, as though they belong.

Once everyone's in, you give motivational, rousing talks about how, together, we can change our destiny and overcome adversity, nothing is impossible (as long as we stick together) - that kind of thing. You have to give people a feeling of superiority against others – you know that the group is right and everyone else is wrong. You have to foster an 'us against them' attitude. Get people to really invest themselves.

The more I thought about it, the more I realised what a great cult leader I'd make. Men did tend to worship me. Not so sure about women, but I don't think Charles Manson's Family was a mixed sex cult either. Men only would be fine.

If I really was maniacal or just morally corrupt, then I could start my own cult. There I go with that high opinion of myself again! I must remember it's not shared by others. Well, not those outside my cultish fantasies anyway. Okay, I appreciate that leading a cult is probably not as easy as I make out here, but I definitely have the requisite superiority complex and bossy nature. I can even use words like "requisite" properly and feel smug about it. But luckily for vulnerable young men around here, it goes against my belief in individual responsibility to encourage other people to become so dependent on me.

Besides, I couldn't stand to have my life taken over like that and having to live with a group of devotees and be the centre of their universe. I feel claustrophobic if another person even sits on a couch beside me. I always hated the idea of being on Big Brother because I couldn't stand having to live with other people. It's the same with jail. I think I'd opt for solitary confinement.

Yes, so there's no way I'd be leading a cult by living in some commune-type arrangement. No. If I was doing any kind of leading, it would just be to ask people for help, using the talents they have. I'd only persuade by waking people up to their plight, telling them how things really are, maybe suggesting how they could use their skills to change things. You know, a quiet protest by ordinary people can be very effective. But I've already established that no-one's going to bother protesting, even me, and that it's pointless because we have no idea who's really running the show anyhow. The word "impotent" springs to mind.

24. PROTEST

I love the origin of the term "Boycott" – where a nasty land agent, Captain Boycott, was ostracised by the people of Ireland to the extent that no-one would speak to him or work for him, shops stopped serving him, and even his mail stopped being delivered. He was completely "sent to Coventry". This silent act of refusal has been effective time and again over the years: look at Rosa Parks, the black civil rights activist, who refused to give up her seat on a bus for a white passenger in the 1950s, leading to the bus strikes where black people refused to travel by bus until they were treated fairly.

I personally have never voted in any type of election. To do so would be to take part in the charade of democracy in this country. If no-one had voted in the US presidential elections at all, there could have been no so-called "stolen elections" in 2000 and 2004 and George W. Bush's election as President would have been readily transparent as a dictatorship. It is only by participating in the process of so-called democracy that we allow ourselves to be used to uphold an unjust system. Boycott the State by refusing to vote at all. What would they do then if no-one voted? Let's all try it and see. Yes, women fought for the right to vote and I should probably be ashamed of myself, but I doubt Pankhurst and her cronies were from the lower classes, or any of them from a minority background.

There's no use having things like a Bank Transfer Day here, not in this town. Well there is, it would be great if people did regularly change their bank accounts, or tried to save through credit unions and regularly changed their utility suppliers – oh yes, that might stop the big businesses becoming too complacent. I doubt it. A lot of people around here struggle to get even a basic bank account and often have no choice but to have one because most benefits nowadays are paid by direct bank transfer.

Anyway, I digress. The bottom line is that I think that people should do their bit, using their talents and resources in silent acts of refusal and protest.

25. HEAD FAKE

In his Last Lecture, the late Professor Randy Pausch talks about how you think you know the purpose of why you are here or what you're taking away from an activity, but come away having learnt something completely different. That sums up my life: I thought that if I worked hard at developing myself as best I could, then one day, my talents would be appreciated by the world and that (this is my ego talking here) I would leave some kind of lasting legacy – nothing spectacular, just a really good book that I'd written; or some great problem that I'd solved and be remembered for.

I also hoped to be living quite comfortably by the time I got to middle age. I'm not talking about living in some mansion (although that would, of course, be great), but to still be living in an ex-council house with bare floorboards and not being able to afford to heat it or replace a broken window or fix the leak in the roof isn't really living up to my ideal…

So why, Randy, am I really here? By chance, at birth, to be the voice of the disenfranchised underclass? No. I can throw a huge tantrum and scream at the top of my lungs about how unfair the world is, but it changes nothing. Little children have been beaten, forced to work long hours in terrible conditions, trained as soldiers, and millions starved to death for centuries. Nothing changes. No-one cares enough to do anything. We are the worker ants or the drones of the bee world.

I know that you probably want to come away from here feeling happier that someone has taken on "the system", and that it can be done; that there is a chance that the underdogs can have their day and fight back against the big companies (and the people behind them) who have everything, while the rest of us struggle. But nothing will change.

I have come to accept that.

I would love it if life was like Fight Club and I was Tyler Durden, fighting against the Establishment, but even if I spent years or even just months of my life recruiting other people and manipulating them into helping bring down the global economy or hitting back at multi-national companies, it wouldn't work. Especially not for me: I'm not that stupid and fatalistic. I prefer a less risky, more realistic approach because, as I've admitted, I am a bit nerdy. But I hope that other people at least wake up a bit and look around them. I think that's possible. Hopefully, more people will realise the huge inequality in the world now. At least that would be a start.

One thing I have learned from going through my past and thinking about these contemporary issues is that we should not be ashamed of our culture. We should not be *made* to feel ashamed of who we are. We are a product of our environment, yet at the same time, we are made to feel as though the underclass sub culture is something to be ridiculed and embarrassed about, just like for generations, we were taught that our Glaswegian accent was bad and the dialect we spoke in was "slang" and wrong and inferior to *proper* English. Who has made us feel second-rate and what are we being judged on? Is it the sum total of our accent; the backgrounds of our acquaintances; our choice of High Street brands; our moral deficiency; lack of work ethic; and a problem with drink and drugs? Or is it our limited lifestyle choices, making do with the resources we have available?

People who at best can expect a job in a supermarket, or working for the council, or in a call centre, whilst spending their lives living in a local authority housing estate in the same town as their parents, are going to end up feeling at least a bit disillusioned and in need of the soporific effects of alcohol or drugs to help them come to terms with that. It's a huge disappointment to have to deal with the realisation that this is as good as your life is going to get, no matter how hard you work.

People want to believe that ordinary nobodies like them can be rich and famous and that all they have to do is want it badly enough and it will be theirs:

"Start cutting out pictures of the things you want and, miraculously, they'll come into your life. Just dream about anything you want and it's yours."

Either that, or you will win the Euro millions. Never mind that it's often been odds of over 56 million-to-one. People cling on to such fantasies because they want to escape from their lives. Give it up! For those of you with the child-like optimism to keep dreaming that somehow, eventually, your time will come, you really will have a better life, a big house, enough money to spend: it is NOT going to happen. A lottery win is NOT pre-ordained in your favour.

This is your reality. Your life is not going to get any better. You are not going to get any richer. You are only going to get older and poorer. Time is running out.

26. WILL TO POWER

I now realise that Nietzsche was right: we should all try to become the very best that we can be, to develop ourselves as much as we can, and to use and share our talents with other people (this is what I think he meant by our "will to power" on the path to becoming the Übermensch).

Writers, actors, artists, poets, film-makers, dancers, comedians, athletes, teachers, scholars, inventors – they are all *doing* and creating and pushing themselves. The person who invented the internet; who designed the micro-chip; who defined evolution; who explained the theory of relativity; those who invented machines that allow us to talk to people miles away, see moving images on screen, give images of our tissues, bones, foetuses; who invented aircraft and vehicles that allow us to fly across the globe or travel to the next town – they have all *given* something. They have all added value to the world.

If we are to live our lives as though we are complying with a universal law, then shouldn't that be to exploit our talents and not other people? We need to wake up and stop being passengers in life as though we're travelling on a train, gawping out the window, mentally commenting on what other people are doing as we trundle along, noses to the glass. We need to stop wasting time on Facebook and watching TV; to stop sitting around, feeling bored or depressed and find something to *do*.

In his book, The War of Art, Steven Pressfield blames a lot of the problems we have as people on not pursuing our inherent talents. As an example, he tells us that Hitler was a painter who did not paint; how great an artist he might have been if he had used his talents. Perhaps he would have been happier and less hell-bent on genocide had he created wonderful art instead of leading his country to war.

And in following that universal law, don't support anything that you would not be happy doing yourself. If you would not be happy raising animals in factory farmed conditions and then slaughtering them, then why pay someone else to do that for you? If you wouldn't feel comfortable ripping off a poor farmer in a developing country somewhere, then don't buy products that won't give that person a decent price for his or her produce. Think about where things come from. Yes, bananas grow on trees, but whose trees? How did they get to that supermarket shelf that you want to buy them from? Think about the people along the journey of each single piece of fruit.

Everything you buy has a history and there are real people behind every purchase you make. You cannot trust the big companies to treat those people fairly, so give them a second of your time to think about their plight. Are you making that person's life better, or worse? Think about the big brands you subsidise – do you know anything about their history, about how they have treated people, anything about their ethical policies? If you don't and if you just buy big brands or stuff from multi-national businesses without a second thought, then you are jointly responsible for the suffering they cause. You might not be making a profit, but you are helping others make a profit from something that you think is wrong.

If no-one bought unethically traded products, it wouldn't be in companies' interests to exploit people.

Don't use the old excuse, "What does one person matter?" or, "I can't change anything". People often level that at me and ask why I even bother being a vegetarian when animals are just going to be killed for meat anyway. They say that I might as well join in, enjoy a steak or a roll and bacon. But if Rosa Parks, or Martin Luther King, Jr., or Mahatma Gandhi, or Nelson Mandela had used the "Why bother? I can't change anything!" excuse then the civil rights of ethnic minorities would be even worse than they are now.

I'm coming around to the idea that quiet protest by ordinary people, simple boycotting, can be very effective. At the very least, I'd say don't be forced into following the herd, if you don't agree with something and if there is something you are fed up with or want to change, at least pledge to do something to spread the word. If you are not sure what your own talent is – if you are convinced you don't have one – then you can still become more aware of how you spend your money and your time.

I need to find out more about ordinary people and their acts of resistance and how individuals have helped change the world. They all have humble beginnings and an ordinary back-story.

Accept that you might never be rich, or famous, or hugely successful, but you can still make a difference.

27. YOUR BEST YOU

Think about this - if it wasn't illegal, if there were no consequences, what would you change? How would you do it? Can you demonstrate this to other people through a song, a piece of art, a film, a story, an improvisation?

Is there a part of yourself that you have neglected – some hobby or pastime that you have always wanted to try, or to devote more time to? Then just do it. No more excuses or putting it off. Don't fritter and waste your life away, never fulfilling any of your dreams, because you are a long time dead. *This* is *your* time.

What can you do, to be all you can be, Übermensch?

REFERENCES

Byrne, R. *The Secret,* Simon & Schuster Ltd (4 Dec 2006)

Dalrymple, T. *Life at the Bottom: The Worldview That Makes the Underclass,* Ivan R Dee, Inc; Reprint edition (8 Mar 2003)

Mohr, B. *The Cosmic Ordering Service,* Hodder Paperbacks (24 Aug 2006)

Nietzsche, F. *Thus Spake Zarathustra,* Wordsworth Editions Ltd; New Ed edition (20 Nov 1997)

Palahniuk, C. *Fight Club* Vintage; New Ed edition (2 Oct 1997)

Pausch, R. The Last Lecture: Lessons in Living, Two Roads (24 Jun 2010)

Printed in Great Britain
by Amazon

60816997R00137